The Man Who Sold Tomorrow

The True Story of Dr. Solomon Trone: The World's Greatest, And Perhaps Only, Revolutionary Salesman

DAVID EVANS

THE MAN WHO SOLD TOMORROW: THE TRUE STORY OF DR. SOLOMON TRONE THE WORLD'S GREATEST & MOST SUCCESSFUL & PERHAPS ONLY REVOLUTIONARY SALESMAN

Copyright ©2019 David Evans. All Rights Reserved.

Published by:
Trine Day LLC
PO Box 577
Walterville, OR 97489
1-800-556-2012
www.TrineDay.com
trineday@icloud.com

Library of Congress Control Number: 2019931484

Evans, David.
The Man Who Sold Tomorrow – 1st ed.
p. cm.
Epub (ISBN-13) 978-1-63424-191-5
Kindle (ISBN-13) 978-1-63424-192-2
Print (ISBN-13) 978-1-63424-190-8
1. Trone, Solomon Abramovich--1872-1969. 2. Electric power -- Russia -- History. 3. Electric power -- General Electric -- History. 4. Expatriate scientists -- 20th century. 5. Central Planning. I. Title

FIRST EDITION
10 9 8 7 6 5 4 3 2 1

Printed in the USA
Distribution to the Trade by:
Independent Publishers Group (IPG)
814 North Franklin Street
Chicago, Illinois 60610
312.337.0747
www.ipgbook.com

Do you want to know who you are? Don't ask. Act! Action will delineate and define you.

– Thomas Jefferson

If you don't design your own life plan, chances are you'll fall into someone else's plan. And guess what they have planned for you? Not much.

– Jim Rohn

Life is a series of natural and spontaneous changes. Don't resist them-that only creates sorrow. Let reality be reality. Let things flow naturally forward in whatever way they like.

– Lao Tzu

CONTENTS

Preface

SPIRITUS MUNDI

At times it seems like there is a spirit at work in the world, drawing us all closer together. It is a global force pushing us into one global community, whether we are conscious of it or not, no matter whom we are or what we believe. Its magnetic pull, will not rest, it can only be resisted, never defeated. As inevitable as death, we are drawn into a world where race, religions, languages, borders and just about anything that can separate people into different groups is becoming increasingly irrelevant. Whether by design or accident it seems unstoppable.

Forced to confront the interconnection of our lives across a global network of different places and persons, we may find ourselves wondering how it all came about. Was there a decision at some point that would make all of our plans in life interconnected and interdependent? Who made that decision? Why was it made? The answer to these questions is not as difficult to find out as you might expect.

Yes, there was a decision made and I can point out exactly who was responsible and why he did it. Without him of course someone else may have made it all possible, and perhaps it was inevitable. But it was not someone else; it was a particular man, whose name was Solomon Pesach Abramovitch Trone. This book is the story of that man and how the world changed because of his decision. That he was in a position to make such a decision was largely luck. Sometimes in his long and remarkable career he was merely the last man standing at a critical juncture where something could be done by someone who knew what to do. You have probably never heard of this man and yet his role is indisputable.

At a specific time and place that force of globalization possessed Trone, who would change the nature of how we live, drawing us all closer together in such a way that we cannot separate ourselves from the global web of interconnections. He made a deal for American businesses and Russian politicians, which not only represented a new way of doing business; it represented a new way of living on the planet. It is a relatively new element that now dominates most aspects of our lives.

Trone unleashed a force that has encompassed the globe, spreading its influence everywhere, connecting us all in one great orchestrated network of plans. It is the first glimmering of a world becoming conscious of itself. A consciousness emerging to direct the development of the world, freeing itself step by step from the irrational; no longer pushed hither and thither, knowing not what we are to do next or why.

There was a specific moment when Trone made the fatal decision that would change the world. To be more precise it was a decision that was created in the moment when all other possibilities for Trone were removed, by an event both horrific and entirely unexpected. That event was the Bloody Sunday Massacre of 1905 in Russia.

Introduction

BLOODY SUNDAY

There must have been for Trone a great sense of shock as the bullets went over the heads of the procession. It was reported that the people in the procession did not expect to be fired upon. The first warning shot probably stopped Trone dead his tracks, as it did most people marching. Like others who have reported being at the event, Trone was probably in a state of disbelief when the second volley was fired into the crowd. Even with the best estimates it's hard to know what happened or how many died. Some estimates say a thousand. To Trone the number of victims he would remember from the massacre was four. Every year to commemorate the day of the massacre, Trone would have four carnations put in a vase. He lost four friends that day, one of whom was his lover.

The event of course was not just critical for Trone. The event was critical to the fall of the Romanov's rule of Russia. It tarnished The Czar's image in the minds of the Russian people. Delegated down the line from the Czar's authority, the order to shoot was never condemned by the Czar, nor were any of those responsible charged with murder. Later selectively grabbed workers were taken by the military, pushed forth on their knees to be told off by the Czar, and then told categorically that he had no choice. The befuddled workers were then sent back to explain to the people how right the Czar had been. This had little effect but to assure many people, particularly Trone, how out-of-touch the government was from the people.

Especially tragic was the nature of the slaughter. As Trone well knew, working for the government and its military, this was not a country unaccustomed to harsh repression and brutality. What really shook people, including Trone, was the surprise of the incident. If you expect something, when it happens, good or bad, you can be prepared for it. But this was odd, odd in a sense that it made no sense.

Trone was a man who prized reason and rationality above anything else. To this event there was no reason, it served no purpose. The Czar's most devoted subjects led by a loyal priest, who was even in the pay of the police force, arrived before the imperial palace to pray for the Czar, on their knees, to pray that the Czar would hear their prayer for better working conditions.

Trone had joined in a procession of workers who were not demanding power, or even making demands. They were hoping just to let the Czar know that things were quite bad, and they wanted to pray for the Czar to be able to do something to help them. What Trone would have seen at the end of the procession was the indiscriminate shooting and stabbing of these same poor subjects of the Czar. As they held Holy Icons and prayed for the Czar's health and the sanctity of his semi-divine Emperorship, they were killed. The whole thing would have been the height of the irrational for Trone, as it was for the vast majority in Russia and the world.

It struck a spark that soon had revolution raging throughout the Russian Empire and turned Trone into a Revolutionary who was eventually imprisoned that year for revolutionary activity. Unable to fully organize the revolution failed. Like Trone, no one was expecting or planning to take power, with no specific plans or unity the revolution fell apart. Revolutionaries, such as Trone, ended up imprisoned. In many cases the revolutionaries ended up shot, tortured and exiled. Russia fell city by city, region by region, back into the Czar's clutches once again.

The 1905 Revolution, though lost, was really just a dress rehearsal for Trone. Like so many others caught up in the uprising of 1905 for Trone this was not the end of anything. It was the beginning of real preparations that would eventually see the end of the Romanov Dynasty. All throughout the

Russian empire, people such as Trone and groups were dedicating themselves to going all the way next time, getting really organized, making alliances, making sure they were prepared take power and keep it. For Trone his connections and preparations would prove perhaps the most pivotal and would have the most ramifications for the world as a whole.

The trigger that started this chain of events, that would start Trone on his career, was something that he should never have been. His incredible career as a Revolutionary Salesman, surely a contradiction in terms, began in a place where he should never have been. He was a director for General Electric's Russian subsidiary and he was a Jew. He had no official business out on a protest march for Russian workers where no Jews were allowed to take part. This is not something strange for Trone however. The most amazing aspect of Trone's life was that he was always where you would not expect him, and where you would expect him he was never there.

He liked to talk and be with friends. On this day of the massacre, on either side of him, they would all be dead from gunshots fired by trained soldiers of the Czar. The march was only for good ethnic Russians who worshipped the Czar as the semi-divine defender of the Orthodox faith. Trone was a Jew and did not worship the Czar. Why was he there? He knew some political activists, probably members of the Social Revolutionary Party, or the Russian Social Democratic Labour Party. The people he knew and the fact he was incredibly social, meant that he would have showed up anyway because his friends were there, not caring if he was supposed to be there or not.

When the bullets hit, the reports say that everyone was in shock initially. The Narva Gate was in front of Trone and in the street behind him there must have been thousands of people crammed in tight, pushing forward. Trone must have felt the push from the people in front and the wild cries, as people panicked realizing what was happening.

Trone would have been in the right place to see the Cossack cavalry marshaling their horses. The charge made at the crowd would have been directly toward where Trone was standing. Either he was watching them as they approached, brandishing their sabres, or more likely he would have been pushing his way out of the crowd to any place of safety.

To most people and probably to Trone, the initial moments of the massacre appeared like a nightmare; as if it could not be happening. The day had been one of hope. For a person who was almost always brimming over with hope it is not hard to imagine that Trone was looking forward to a successful conclusion to the procession. The people would get to present their petition to the Czar. But here Trone was staring death in the face, death in the form of a cavalry charge of sabre wielding Cossacks.

Trone never quite recovered from 1905, his whole life was somehow predicated by it, framed by it. The measure of his worth until the end of his days was in respect to the revolutionaries he knew when he was young who died in the massacre. The slaughter of 1905's Bloody Sunday created for Trone a moment when fear melted into a certainty that death and the necessity to act were one and the same. To die was nothing compared to the essential act of truly living for something meaningful. He would constantly offer himself as a sacrifice for beliefs that he shared with those friends who died.

Trone was a student of philosophy, and he had learned that the purpose of philosophy was learning how to be prepared to die, again and again, in situations throughout the world during six decades of constant travelling. Never can the word fear be found in any of his writings, his letters or his conversations recalled by friends. In learning how to die well, he learned how to live well. It was as if he expected to die, had been prepared for it by the death of his friends in 1905.

He faced danger after danger in order to fight for the ideals of those he had loved and had died on that day. He never forgot them, nor was their place in his life ever anything but central, they were the foundation of his life, they encompassed his every act. It was to be, by any standard, an incredible life.

He began at that moment a strange career where he travelled in Siberia alone by dogsled, was perhaps the only Jew ever chauffeured in comfort to over thirty concentration camps and slept in a luxury hotel every night during that tour, he evaded the FBI for forty years, he witnessed his friends tried and executed by Stalin, and at one point he got to sit strapped into an electric chair with the metal plate on his head in Sing-Sing prison. He was a man staring death, catastrophe and hardship in the face for most of his life from 1905 on, never flinching in fear, never shying away from the struggle.

What happened to Trone that day in 1905? Before that day he was on way up the corporate ladder. His political days were passed and he had not participated in anything seriously political for almost a decade. Then there was 1905. They had all marched in what was expected to be a loyal procession, only smaller groups such as the Bolsheviks gave any warning that this was a suicide.

Most adventures begin with a critical decision by one man to face the trials of nature or society. As if he was a single point of light in the darkness. This is the picture of man alone, a Robinson Crusoe moment; the hero deciding to pit his wits and determination against the world, against nature. Not so with Trone. In the gloriously happy days before 1905, he had become quite content, and had become a relatively affluent executive. The time however was out of joint, and he was created to put things right as a revolutionary at that moment at the massacre. Using his wit and skill he was driven forth by an event that was not of his choosing.

He had a wife, child, lover, and plenty meetings with his friends in coffee shops to discuss politics. He once had burning ideals, the revolutionary ideals of his youth, and had once even got arrested. As punishment he had to serve in the Czar's army for a few months. But those days were long gone. Now he was comfortably numb to the burning desire to make a stand. To him was allotted the poison of hope, that everything would be okay and all the problems could be resolved just by asking politely for it. Well all those with his sense of optimism gathered together and asked for it, and they received something they did not expect.

Do great historical forces create men or do men create great historical forces? Of course it is both. The time and place of the massacre created Trone, he moved from that moment inextricably to make a deal with the Bolsheviks that would change the world. He felt at the time that no other group could be trusted to act decisively enough to change Russia permanently, from a medieval state where blind illusions ruled a land of slaughter and famine.

If history is the nightmare that we are trying collectively to awake from, Trone tried to wake us all up a little earlier. As we shall see the world as a whole desired to keep sleeping, engrossed in its dreams, that are no more than illusions, for just a little longer.

Perhaps the greatest illusion, truly the only real enemy of Trone was that the individual does not need facts to live, to act, that somehow his will makes reality. If you are powerful enough truth is a beggar at your court and can be spurned. Truth seen as an irrelevant affectation of the weak, nothing can be outside the possibility of the truly great man. The will to power is the will to truth; you create the truth out of the greatness of your power. If we want it so, then it is so.

Trone was in the business of giving people power, power that tipped the balance in the great struggles between nations. It was the power of rational thought, independent thinking, looking reality in the face, seeing things the way they are before us, not as we would have them be.

Before the massacre, Trone seemed very comfortable with the autocracy, with the Czar, and his comfortable existence with his dalliance in polite politics, it was a very pleasant life. He electrified the Czar's military installations, built the electrical power stations for the idle rich in Moscow and St. Petersburg, who lived off the labour of the peasants who starved ignorantly living a barbaric existence. Trone was a servant of the powerful, with illusions to being a child of the enlightenment, a humanitarian lover of the people and true rationalist.

In 1905 with the dead surrounding him, mowed down by rifle fire and hacked like meat in a butchers shop by the Cossacks, he was forced to see a version of reality that had escaped him before this point. Forced to look at the truth before him, he would spend a life time never allowing himself to look away, a persistence to see in all the horror what any of us would rather not know. Before 1905 he fled from the truth, after 1905 the truth was his constant pursuit.

Chapter 1

LOOKING FOR THE HEART OF THE REVOLUTION

The View from Hampstead Heath

Britain is not such an ugly place for an American such as Dr. Solomon Trone to go and die of old age. Instead of facing the electric chair like his friends the Rosenburgs he was forcibly retired. The place of his enforced retirement happened to be Hampstead. The exact place was right next to Hampstead Heath, in a tastefully decorated spacious flat, replete with original drawings by Kathy Kollwitz and Mayakovski hanging on the walls.

From the living room in this place one can look out onto the Heath and get an almost uninterrupted view looking down on most of London. If any of us were cast out of where we live now to such an exile in Hampstead, to live out the rest of our days surrounded by family and friends, it is doubtful any one of us would have much cause to complain. This is not how one expects America to treat those it suspects of Capital Treason. After all, Hampstead is long way from Guantanamo Bay.

Even in 1953 Hampstead England was hardly the torment of the damned; now of course it's one of the richest places on earth. Not far in the distance, on the other side of the Heath is the last resting place of Karl Marx. On this side is the last residence of a man who helped make the events possible that put Marx on a pedestal for almost a century. Foolish perhaps, a dreamer certainly, he was an engineer, a revolutionary and the best damn salesman General Electric ever had; here lived the spectacular and some would say romantic and passionate Dr. Solomon Trone.

In a long game of a cat and mouse, or, to be more accurate, spy versus spy, Trone had one opponent who hunted him off and on through four decades of his life. J. Edgar Hoover first became wise to Trone shortly after

World War One, when as a young Justice Department employee he created a list on which Trone's name was included. It was not, however, until after World War Two that Hoover was presented with a dossier of Solomon Trone's industrious pursuits, to which he remarked with trembling enthusiasm, "This is an amazing story[1]." Trone, always one step ahead, was more than aware by this point that Hoover was closing in on him.

J. Edgar Hoover when he had just got out of law school had begun a career with the Department of Justice by compiling a list of dangerous radicals[2]. Like the list sung about in the Gilbert and Sullivan operetta the Mikado, it was a "little list" of "society offenders" whom, if executed "would not be missed." And just like the list in the Mikado some have speculated, "it really does not matter who you put upon the list," because the real purpose of the list was primarily to calm the fears of the American public.

What the American public feared was both the real and imaginary threats from anarchists and others. If this meant taking the innocent with the guilty J. Edgar Hoover did not appear to mind. Officially the list was supposed to comprise those who were considered a danger to the state during the Red Scare that swept America at the end of the First World War and into the 1920s. Like the lists of suspected communists created during the McCarthyism of the 1950s, this earlier list contained a lot more than a collection of names of those assumed to be guilty of treason.

At this time of Red Scare hysteria, when bombs, set by self-proclaimed anarchists, were exploding Wall Street and rumours abounded of foreign agents invading America it was not a good time to be a known political radical. It was J. Edgar Hoover's job to make a list of all the radicals so they could be monitored, captured and then dealt with appropriately, especially as it turned out if they were Jews and Russians living in New York[3]. These two groups were of particular interest to Hoover.

The Espionage List based upon the Espionage Act was broad enough to cast a very wide net including many who were neither dangerous nor politically radical. The Espionage List brought together a diverse set of people. It contained those who had wanted a German victory in the First World War, and pacifists who wanted to end the same war. It named also union activists who had no opinions about the war but whose motives were simply to build "One Big Union." The list even contained older ladies who started a "Knitting Cooperative" not realizing to do so was like declaring to J. Edgar Hoover that they were bomb throwing anarchists working directly for the Kaiser of Germany. Why? Because their organization contained the word "cooperative" which Hoover thought was a code word for anarchist.

Like every good drama, needing its cast of heroes and villains, not everyone on the Espionage List however was innocent. There were, of course the usual anarchist suspects who did advocate violent actions and who were still at large. These people were also prepared to take their war against the state and the rich to a higher level.

Solomon Trone, playing multiple roles, was not only on that list, he was also actively pursued in New York and the surrounding area by agents of the newly formed FBI who were determined to find him. His name had been given by several informants, who claimed that Trone was either a Bolshevik revolutionary or a Czarist agent, depending upon the political inclination of the informant.

To the left-wing socialist oriented Lieutenant Governor of New York, George Lunn, Trone was a dangerous agent of the Czar[4], while to others, such as a Russian exile devoted to the Czar Trone was in the pay of the Bolsheviks aiming to overthrow the United States government by force[5]. To the 24-year-old Hoover, Trone well and truly deserved to be on the list, although he may not have known exactly why. The investigation of Trone that started in 1917 was left incomplete. As we shall see later Trone evaded the investigation in America until 1921, then he escaped to work in Berlin where GE had shifted its headquarters for working with Russia[6].

After almost four decades J. Edgar Hoover had almost forgotten about Trone. This in itself is interesting. Trone was never far away from the antennae of the U.S. government's numerous intelligence agencies. Trone himself even said he had been interviewed by every intelligence agency the U.S. government had several times over. Trone also made it a point to visit the U.S. Consuls and Ambassadors un-announced whenever and wherever he traveled abroad, to discuss politics without dissimulation and give his opinion regarding world affairs. The U.S. embassy officials were invariably glad to see him and took his advice and opinion with a good deal of enthusiasm. One American secret service agent in the Middle East was so taken aback by the extremely talkative hard-left radical, Trone, that he could hardly believe him to be an agent of the Soviet Union.

Of course the intelligence agencies especially the FBI would have been well advised to read a popular comedy book of the day. That is, of course, if they had known which popular comic novel to read. Unlike others who were accused of being spies or foreign agents Trone gave his opinions extensively in a popular book of the day which was read by millions and was available in many languages. He was the major figure in a book about the United States written by famous Russian writers. Trone took no steps to disguise himself or his opinions which were now widely available due to this book. It is impossible to conceive that Trone was a spy considering how open he was to the world generally.

Little Golden America by Ilf and Petrov was published in English in both America and England in the 1930s and again in the 1940s. The novel gave Trone a starring role which allowed him to give a full account of himself and gave a platform for his political opinions. Appearing in the role of Mr. Adams, Trone and his brilliant wife Florence gave the two top Russian writers of the day a road trip review of the United States from New York to San Francisco and back. Alexander Ilf even said that Mr. Adams was Trone in his published letters and journals. There was no attempt to disguise Trone or his opinions.

Perhaps it may be reasoned Trone had hidden from the two Russian writers his intimate knowledge of the powerful political circles that he was familiar with in the Soviet Union and America? Nothing could be further from the truth. It was Trone's vast knowledge of the powerful political circles, and his personal connection to them, in both the Soviet Union and the United States that was the real substance of *Little Golden America* not simply the road trip.

Shortly after they had got to know Trone for the first time the writers Ilf and Petrov said something very unusual. They stated after their first full conversation with Dr. Trone that they were convinced they knew absolutely nothing at all about how the Soviet Union or America was run by its leaders. They said before Trone they were innocents, they "were like new born calves." Trone told them just about anything and everything, much of which is recorded in the novel.

Well into his sixties Trone travelled across the United States with the Russian writers. His wife had to drive both him and the writers as he could no longer drive. He could not drive because he was unable to concentrate due to his relentless and increasing desire for endless conversation. He talked and talked from one coast to the other and back again. At one point Ilf and Petrov even pretended to be asleep so as to escape the conversation of Dr. Trone. Ilf and Petrov discovered the trouble with Trone was not getting him to talk, and prying the important secrets out of him; the trouble was getting to grips with the sheer volume of knowledge that Trone was freely given to talk about.

It is not that Trone was a boring conversationalist, far from it, everyone found him fascinating. Trone was in turn fascinated by life and world around him. With several science degrees, having circled the globe several times, and visited dozens of countries, he was relentless in his desire to know the world as it was and build a better world out of it. Due to his unusual education, which we shall look at later, Trone's vision grew straight out of the Eighteenth Century Enlightenment. He wanted to see a world re-founded on rational principles like those set forth by his heroes Voltaire, Kant and Hegel. Much more than this though, he saw himself on a mission to enlighten himself and enlighten everyone else as well.

Enlightening or to define it a little further, supplying a broader rational understanding of the world is just what he did. He engaged others in conversation to such a broad degree that it seemed to some as if he had been compiling scientifically an understanding of all the major social groupings on the planet, as if he were a latter day Darwin searching the world for specimens of animal and plant life. With the same vigorous pleasure he would engage Indian farmers, American presidents, and obscure Russian religious sect members in conversation. Trone was at home both in the corridors of power and the homes of the powerless. He crossed the many degrees of social separation that divide the world up and down, as easily and as effortlessly as if those degrees of separation did not exist.

This is perhaps the reason why Trone is so unknown today, and his contribution to history so little recognized. Fixing Trone in time and place, pinning him with a description of the group to which he belonged is futile. Bolshevik, revolutionary, advisor to U.S. presidents, scientist, salesman, dreamer and realist, all these and more are just as equally applicable and inapplicable to Trone.

Hidden in plain view Trone said exactly what was on his mind, when and where ever he chose. Only at very rare moments did Trone ever conceal his aims. At most he merely did not say those things that no one would have believed anyway. Such a person defies description, and therefore is left without a description, undocumented precisely because he refused to be limited in what he said and did.

Intelligence agents and historians look for where his loyalties lay, who paid him, what were the ideals he would die for. In looking for these things, the search comes up empty. His homeland was the future; his loyalty was to an enlightened world that did not exist, a world without borders, without leaders and almost certainly without the ideological certainties of those who were investigating him.

Catching the Big Fish

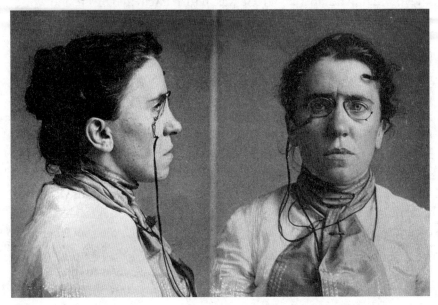

❝ …blood-curdling and incoherent stories have been circulated about me, it is no wonder that the average human being has palpitation of the heart at the very mention of the name Emma Goldman."[7] This was the description that Emma Goldman, or Red Emma as she was known, gave of herself when asked by a popular newspaper. Today it seems that the name of Emma Goldman is mixed with ten parts fantasy, one part truth. In the movie "Reds" one gets the picture of a rather dour and dedicated pessimist who unequivocally condemns anything and anyone that she disapproves of. Such is the reality about Emma that this picture could not be further from the truth.

In her day, she was a star of international renown. Young, beautiful, smart, she was so full of drama and theatrical panache that she charmed America and was considered by many to be the best show in town. Crammed to the walls with spectators, people of all political stripes would fill theatres and chant "Emma, Emma, Emma," banging on the walls, stamping on the floor, just to hear her speak. They wanted to hear what she was famous for; something deliciously mind blowingly radical about "Free Love" or violently taking on the immense power of the Robber Barons and Politicians.

Perhaps this was because she was so passionate, with such a mischievous look in her eyes whenever she spoke on stage; there was something mesmerizing about this beautiful young Russian immigrant when she engaged the public. She burned with an intensity of purpose. No dramatic opportunity to say something radically disturbing was wasted. When the president was assassinated she publically said she was glad, not caring about the danger it put her in. When the postmaster general wanted to stop her distributing birth control advice to women, she called him a eunuch. Whether she was physically whipping a male opponent in public or advocating Free Love on the stages of New York, Emma Goldman was a sensation. Conventional wisdom, conventional morality were thrown out the window in what she saw as a battle for the soul of humanity and in particular the struggle for the liberation of the female soul; to love and live on her own terms in a world that was full of oppression.

By 1917 Emma Goldman was well known, as famous as she was infamous. She was brought to trial with her one time lover and fellow Anarchist Alexander Berkman. They were both part of a group of people rounded up and arrested earlier in the year, just when America had entered the First World War. The defendants were on trial for resisting America's entry into the war. They were, according to the police, encouraging men not to enlist and fight in the war. In truth, Emma saw no reason to become "a party to the world slaughter."

Emma's defence was impeccable. Even the judges, so keen and convinced of her guilt before, during and after the trial, could not help but say how impressed they were with it. Conducting her own legal defence, the arguments she made were concise; she spoke with effect and clarity and never indulged in anything beneath the conduct of the most respectable of lawyers. The judges even lamented how sad it was that Emma was against them, she could have been so valuable to state and the world of business if she had only chosen a different path.

Her closing speech is surely one of the most defining in her career. The speech was such a clear and comprehensive statement of her political philosophy that she thought the jail term imposed but a small price to pay for having had the opportunity to so fully speak her mind to an American public who were following the trial closely. To Emma what she was being tried for was her definition of what America was and what it should be. To Emma, the America she loved was the America of Freedom and vast dreams of a better life.

> "Our patriotism is that of the man who loves a woman with open eyes. He is enchanted by her beauty, yet he sees her faults. So we, too, who know America, love her beauty, her richness, her great

possibilities; we love her mountains, her canyons, her forests, her Niagara, and her deserts – above all do we love the people that have produced her wealth, her artists who have created beauty, her great apostles who dream and work for liberty – but with the same passionate emotion we hate her superficiality, her cant, her corruption, her mad, unscrupulous worship at the altar of the Golden Calf."[8]

To the broad mass of the people in the United States at this time, America was about being patriotic and answering the call when necessary to fight for a version of "Freedom" that was not so vast, nor so dream-like and Utopian as Emma Goldman would have liked.

It was because Emma Goldman was so outspoken and so unconventional that she was both popularly entertaining and unfortunately constantly getting the attention of a government looking for radicals to arrest. The government had marked Emma as the "Big Fish" who was the source and the center of all that America feared during the Red Scare.

Even Emma recognized this and said so at her trial. Mocking the extravagant persecution at the hands of the state, her arrest looked like a spectacle fit for the "Barnum and Bailey circus," replete with gun wielding heroes to arrest her and Alexander Berkman, "...quietly at work at their desks, wielding not a sword, nor a gun or a bomb, but merely their pens! Verily, it required courage to catch such big fish."

Emma though had not quite understood what was going on, and those who had arrested her were equally off the mark in targeting Emma Goldman as the ringleader they were looking for. Nothing here was quite what it appeared.

Little did Emma Goldman know about the young law school graduate J. Edgar Hoover. Early in his career he had created a list, of which Emma Goldman was put at the head. She was the supposed head of a conspiracy to overthrow the government of the United States. A strange belief had taken over many people in the U.S. Justice department. The belief was that the Revolution in Russia was orchestrated by former residents of New York. Somehow the revolutionaries in Russia and the radicals on the Lower East Side were connected in a global conspiracy[9].

While Emma Goldman was completely innocent of orchestrating revolution in Russia and of planning to overthrow the government in the U.S., the Justice Department was not, in fact, completely mistaken in their suspicions. Emma Goldman, however, was not the person they should have been looking for.

If the Justice department had paid a little more attention to the court speech of Emma Goldman they might even have been given a clue as to where to look for the "Big Fish" of the global conspiracy. Emma Goldman, perhaps innocently perhaps not, had suggested that the authorities might try raiding the offices of the Robber Barons and in particular J. P. Morgan if they were looking for the real criminal "Big Fish."

If the Justice Department had raided the offices of J. P. Morgan at this point they would have found references to a certain resident of New York, a Russian who was traveling back and forward from New York to the Revolutionary hot spots of Russia. That person was named Solomon Trone.

If they had been able to track Trone effectively they would have found he was part of a very large organization dedicated to helping the revolutionary government of Russia. This organization was also bent upon bringing a good part of the Russian Revolution back to America.

Whether anyone realized it or not in the court room where Emma Goldman was tried, the "Big Fish" was not only free to organize revolution he was at that moment about to land the biggest business deal in the history of the world. The deal itself that Trone would eventually broker and sign on behalf of General Electric with the Bolsheviks would provide the essential power necessary for the completion of Lenin's ultimate goal of the Revolution: The electrification of Russia. As Lenin had said, "Communism is Socialism plus Electricity."

To tell the story of the real connection between New York and Revolutionary Petrograd, suspected but never really understood by the Department of Justice, we have to follow the wanderings of a very different revolutionary from Emma Goldman. That person was Solomon Trone (Picture left, standing at the back), a man who actually shared a personal enmity with Emma.

Trone's world was far from the prison cells crammed with Russian Jewish radicals like Emma Goldman. The real American life line to the Russian Revolutionaries did not come from the slums of New York's Lower East. It came from such places as the class rooms of Yale and Harvard and the social soirees of New York's high society. How that help was established, how history was changed forever because of it, is entirely due to the efforts of the extraordinary Solomon Trone, whose good fortune put him in the right place at the right time to irrevocably change the course of history.

Three Men in a Boat

The American anarchist bombing campaign of 1920 had almost succeeded in taking out J. P. Morgan Jr.'s Wall Street Office, and much of Wall Street besides[10]. Morgan's empire of Capital was seen by some as the pro-war defender of the moneyed interests and therefore the enemy of radicals everywhere[11]. In a sense, of course, this was correct. J. P. Morgan Jr. was a supporter of the war against Germany and did support the rights of capitalists to operate without restraint[12]. J. P. Morgan Jr., and the corporations he controlled were not however mere combatants in a class war. They were much more than this.

Owning such extensive financial interests meant defending his turf against other powerful organizations and individuals. It was a seemingly trivial matter involving industrial patents in the electrical industry that brought it in conflict with the Czar's government.

Simply put: By 1916 the Czar's government had transgressed against the inviolate rights of American corporations and financial interests by illegally obtaining industrial patents. Possibly without knowing it, the Czar's government had gained possession of industrial patents that were owned through various subsidiaries and holding companies by J. P. Morgan Jr.[13]. How this had happened was due to the necessities of war, the complex interlocking network of Morgan's corporations and elements that were quite accidental.

Patent protection was very sensitive and a very important, if not the most important, factor in Morgan's enterprises, particularly with the Electric Industry. With this industry GE had the most aggressive strategy for patent protection and had deeper pockets than any of its competitors for litigation. Of over 600 hundred patents General Electric litigated in this period, only around 300 were valid[14]. The key was to litigate so aggressively as to scare competitors into submission. Whether the patents' rights were genuinely owned by G.E. or not no one would dare to match the legal cost of making a challenge in the courts.

The Czar's government seized German electrical patents because the Czar was at war with Germany. As the Czar was at war with Germany, seizing the property of the German enemy in Russian territory, such as patents owned by German corporations in Russia, was perfectly fine and well within the rules of war, as they saw it. As the Czar's government was unaware of who ultimately owned the patents they were probably unprepared for the consequences of their action. They had stepped on the toes of someone they really should not have.

The steel toes of JP Morgan and General Electric were not ones to reckon with easily. The major allied combatants, England, France and Russia, were all heavily in debt to J. P. Morgan Jr.[15]. Morgan had financial interests in Germany also, such as the General Electric subsidiary A.E.G.

Like many of the big money houses of the period the First World War was a great and global engine for the accumulation of profit, as Bolshevik Lenin had pointed out[16]. J. P. Morgan would often make clear his immense appreciation for the war with open, public and frequent displays of patriotism and support of the allied troops[17]. For J. P. Morgan Jr. his patriotism was entirely synchronized to his investments.

What the Czar had obviously failed to realize, not looking at it from Morgan's point of view was that the war was primarily for the benefit of those with large amounts of money. Perhaps, if this had dawned on the Czar, the world would be a much different place today. It's impossible to say, of course, and unlikely that the Czar would have done so. Also, it would have taken a monumental imagination at that time to have envisioned the consequences of seizing the German patents.

The Russian Electrical Company had the exclusive rights to the German patents before the war through its connection with A.E.G. both, of course, were affiliates of the General Electric Company. G. E. in turn was affiliated with the investments of J. P. Morgan Junior[18]. The Russian Electrical Company protested when the patents were seized by the Czar's government; its rights had been violated and it called on its head office in New York to do something about it[19].

For the Russian Electrical Company to have let the issue go would have been disastrous. These patents were designs for advanced industrial technology. The Czar's government could and probably would give the patents to other Russian corporations. With a more advanced industry Russia could build better weapons and equipment and thereby win the war, so they hoped. Winning the war however was a secondary consideration for the Russian Electrical Company. The Czar's government had effectively destroyed the monopoly on the patents that A.E.G. had shared with the Russian Electrical Company. When Morgan's executive's got the call from Russia, they were equally motivated to act.

The response from New York was to send three men who would travel to Russia via Vancouver, Canada in December of 1916. These persons were Thomas Nelson Perkins, one of the top lawyers for J. P. Morgan Jr.'s financial interests, a very well connected New York Frenchman named Maurice Oudin and a Russian with radical politics named Solomon Trone.

Perkins was from one of the oldest and richest families of Boston. Before the Civil War the Perkins family had made its money first from the Slave Trade in Haiti and then as drugs smugglers, selling opium in China[20]. Through the Civil War, and as Boston developed into an industrial center, the Perkins parlayed their capital into railroad interests[21]. By the end of the 19th century these interests were important enough to be bought out by Morgan[22].

The latest scion of the family, T. N. Perkins was not so much interested in making money as he was in academic pursuits. He was a sophisticated, highly intelligent and a persuasive lawyer[23]. It was said that he had a knack for cheering people up in the most difficult of situations with his blunt and deadpan humour. In the First World War when the Generals and military bureaucrats in Washington became depressed because of the loss of human life Perkins never did. He took a long and cold view of history and the situation. Perkins always had a joke handy, albeit full of gallows humour; that usually lifted the Generals out of their gloom.

He was one of Boston's top lawyers for a good reason. He had a doctoral degree in the study of law. Despite being well placed and with all the requisite skills and qualifications for success he had relatively few ambitions. He was seemingly content to do merely whatever task J. P. Morgan Jr. or his other employers assigned. This combined with his tremendous physical stamina, made Perkins the best person to send to Russia. Later, Perkins would be the favor ed pick for jobs at the State Department as well. Indeed, it is interesting to note that the objectives of the State Department and J. P. Morgan Jr. often proved to be surprisingly similar. When tasks were assigned for Perkins it was difficult to tell who he was working for or if he was working for both parties at the same time.

The second of the team, Maurice Oudin was born of French parents in New York and his step-father was a Police Justice[24]. Maurice was an upwardly mobile professional and his mobility largely came from his charming manners which had helped him to marry the daughter of the Secretary of the Treasury[25]. He was a very affable, kind person of apparently no particular ambition for power or any discernable political affiliation.

The third of the company, Solomon Trone, was a different kind of traveler entirely. He was the maternal grandson of a Rabbi from the Russian Empire; he was secular and highly political. He was born in what is now Latvia where he had gained his political convictions while a student. Although Trone looked a little chunky, he was in tremendously good physical condition and was well known for his qualities of hard work and endurance.

Trone also had politically radical ambitions. His radicalism had the backing of General Electric's Chief Engineer, C. P. Steinmetz who had given his own radical political doctrine in the form of a book, *America in the New Epoch*[26], to Trone previous to his journey[27]. The book outlined Steinmetz's belief that the introduction of electrical power in industry would change the political economic structure of the world. Steinmetz also suggested what possible new roles America would play in that new world order.

What did Solomon Trone think of Steinmetz's philosophy? That is unknown but Trone was a professed Marxist, and one of his most valued possessions was a signed picture of Steinmetz. Although the two did not share exact ideological positions, they did agree on some important points: The Czar had to be overthrown; Russia had to be modernized; Capitalism, as it was known at the beginning of the twentieth century, had to be abolished to make way for something better.

Trone was in no way your average engineer. He was arrested as a student for political radicalism and sentenced to "serve" for a time in the Czar's military. Throughout his life he was committed to the same radical ideals of his youth. Like many Russians he had taken part in the political events of the 1905 uprising and had been arrested.

Trone had not been lucky. Trone had lost three close friends in the conflict, including his lover, who was standing beside him in a demonstration when she was killed. It was clear to Trone he had only narrowly escaped death; every day after the massacre he would say was a gift. If his life was a gift Trone intended to give 100 percent of it to his political ideals.

When the three J. P. Morgan Jr. officials embarked on their journey from New York they would face something that none were prepared for, not even the politically radical Trone: Out-right revolution.

Trone and his J. P. Morgan Jr. comrades started their journey to Russia by first traveling via the Canadian Pacific Railway across the Canadian Prairies[28]. Somewhere, most likely near the Alberta foothills, their train was stopped under massive winter storms and snow drifts. They were able to cable a message to the General Electric head office for help. They patiently waited. Trone had been the one selected to give his life for the others if help did not arrive in time[29]. Luckily, for him, it did.

They arrived in Vancouver and from there, made their way to Vladivostok via Yokahama and Shanghai on the ship the Empress of Russia. The ship had just finished working the Red Sea for the British Imperial Navy. Now it had been given back temporarily to its owners, the Canadian Pacific company. It was a grand ship, top of the line at the time, and could travel the Pacific in just ten days[30]. Of course Trone, Perkins and Oudin were traveling first class[31].

When they reached Vladivostok, it was quite clear to the party that the situation they were getting into was neither straightforward nor particularly safe. Perkins had not been happy to embark on the journey from the beginning, and had to be convinced by his friend and legal colleague, the future president of G.E., Owen D. Young[32]. If Young and Perkins had not shared such a close friendship, it is doubtful Perkins would have made the journey.

After a brief stop in Shanghai China, where civil disorder was rampant with the fall of the Qing Dynasty, the group arrived in Vladivostok Russia. Once in Russia, they were witness to that country's own social disorders. Here law and order was also breaking down, to the point where an internal conflict seemed imminent – even revolution appeared possible. Russia's war against Germany was a disaster and this in turn exacerbated Russia's extensive pre-existing internal problems.

Their train ride through Russia would have been a relatively rapid fifteen days and comparatively luxurious[33]. While food was becoming a scarcity for many people in Russia, it certainly was not for the representatives of General Electric. At every stop of the train they took on board food especially prepared for them. Every day, at every meal Trone, Oudin and Perkins feasted like kings. Even a new employee for the U.S. consulate in Petrograd, Henry Waterman traveling in the next adjacent car was disturbed by such a feast in a land of famine.

On what was perhaps a humanitarian mission, Waterman was sent by the State Department with a large container of shoes, underpants and other items for German prisoners of war held in Russia; this was one of Waterman's first diplomatic assignments[34]. Trone made friends with Waterman at this time[35]. Waterman joined them for the rest of the journey.

They would spend their days in discussions. Trone was a modern day Socrates who loved to listen and discourse with anyone about everything.

Unlike Socrates, however, Trone did not irritate his companions but would put them at ease and they would find themselves talking unreservedly. His genius for conversation was so remarkable his personality was used as the basis for a character in a famous Russian book, *Little Golden America*.

Perkins, Oudin and Waterman, far from being displeased, apparently enjoyed passing the time in the company of Trone[36]. Whatever their discussions were on the journey, it is clear that when they arrived in Petrograd they were fast friends and would remain so for the rest of their lives. A good, well-connected friend is exactly what each of them needed when they got to Petrograd, a city in the grip of social disorder and revolution. Perkins could not have had a better friend than Trone, a man who knew most of the leaders of the myriad of groups taking control of Petrograd, and all the other major cities throughout the Russian Empire[37]. In short, Trone had all the right connections to make deals with those who had just taken power.

Because of Trone's affable nature, his easy going manner, and his desire to know and speak to everyone – high and low, young and old, male and female – Trone crossed political boundaries easily, and he was not in the least sectarian in his outlook. Although it was rumoured that he had once been a Menshevik, the opposite faction to Lenin's Bolsheviks in the Russian Democratic Labour Party, it seems unlikely that such a man as Trone could ever restrict himself to following one particular party line[38].

For Perkins, his luck must have seemed incredible. Surely the last thing these groups taking control would have worried about was the knotty legal issue of such seeming minutiae as light bulb patents involving numerous subsidiaries of subsidiaries, all locked up in holding companies owned by an American capitalist. But, to General Electric's amazement, within a month Perkins had sorted out an agreement restoring the rights of the patents back to General Electric's subsidiaries and cabled the results of his negotiations to the New York headquarters[39]. How he did this so quickly and easily was a mystery to the G.E. headquarters, and from that point forward Perkins was considered the "Russian Expert"[40].

Perkins, however, did not see it this way. When he sent his bill for services rendered, he added a note that perhaps it should be the General Electric Company sending him a bill not the other way around. As Perkins pointed out when he billed G.E. in late 1917, things had changed radically in Russia; presumably he was referring to Lenin's subsequent rise to power in the October Revolution. One may ask why should the October Revolution affect who billed whom? Owen D. Young answering for General Electric assured Perkins that everything was exactly as it should be.

For the groups taking power, the advantages of making a deal with G.E. were clear. G.E. and those organizations it was affiliated with were important suppliers of parts and machinery to industry. If the change in government was to survive it would need a stable industry. As Russian industry had already disastrously declined, restarting the industry was of critical importance.

Perhaps also Trone's fluency in three languages (German, Russian and English), his ability to talk with just about anyone and his political credentials made the deal not merely possible but, so they all hoped at the time, highly beneficial to all parties.

It is certain that more than the recognition of patent rights had been offered by the new people in power to General Electric. As we shall see, this other secret agreement would be the start of a long term profitable relationship between the Russian government and General Electric. It also was for a project much larger, an agreement to build what would become the foundations for the power of the future Soviet Union. For Trone personally this was a great success both professionally and politically.

While helping Perkins with the patent dispute Trone got wrapped up in the events of the ongoing political changes. Trone was seen by Oudin driving an ambulance for the wounded combatants in the street fighting of Petrograd. It is reasonable to presume that Trone knew that the new government in power needed help, if it was to bring Russia out of the war. Trone had many contacts with these people. Some of these connections were with the powerful Petrograd Soviet[41]. While some were looking to the west to make a deal with the Germans to get Lenin out of Switzerland, Trone was looking to the east, traveling via Siberia back to New York.

According to the FBI reports, Trone was an active radical almost from the moment he landed in the United States in 1912. A frequent visitor to the radical socialist meetings on the Lower East Side in New York, Trone was known within the immigrant community as a political radical. In General Electric's headquarters in Schenectady Trone was known for his politically radical conversations, some of the contents of which were copied in letters to the FBI warning them of the dangerous radical that Trone was[42].

Knowing the New York radical community the way he did, and having a politically sympathetic management at General Electric, Trone in Petrograd in 1917 wanted to return to New York. By doing so Trone hoped to bring much needed support from New York to what he saw as an incomplete revolution.

Russia was still in a war that was crushing the life out its people, and now it was being run by the elite in the Provisional Government who could not act decisively except to preserve their own power. If they could not act to get Russia out of the war, Trone knew people who would. When he and Perkins wrapped up their work involving the German patents with the Provisional Government in March 1917 they decided to return to New York via Vladivostok, Shanghai and Vancouver, the same way as they had come[43].

Although the journey across the Trans-Siberian railway, through China and then by boat to Vancouver was unremarkable, considering an empire was collapsing and there was civil unrest in China, getting off the boat in Vancouver was to prove rather a difficult and long process. A British officer in charge of a Chinese labour detachment being sent to dig trenches and do other physical work for the British military in France had risen in mutiny on board the ship[44]. Not satisfied with his troops, the officer had taken to physically beating them, which had caused the mutiny. As if the mutiny was not enough, there was also an outbreak of the mumps that made the quarantine of passengers necessary[45]. When Trone and Perkins finally did disembark from the boat, it was May the 10th 1917[46].

During the extended wait on board the Empress of Russia, Trone had the opportunity to talk with a writer named Walter Weyl. According to an account given many years later, Trone was full of political zeal at the possibilities that the change in government represented[47]. His work as a General Electric engineer seemed as a very secondary concern to that of the events of the time. FBI and port records show that Trone would spend the next four years traveling between Petrograd and the General Electric offices in Schenectady New York.

When Perkins arrived back he went straight to G.E. headquarters. There he may have been surprised to learn the soon to be International G.E. President Gerard Swope had just left for Petrograd – no doubt, his going, was based upon the telegrams Perkins had sent from there[48]. Due to delays and the urgency of the situation Perkins had missed meeting Swope by a matter of days.

Endnotes

1   (Federal Bureau of Investigation 1945)
2   (Jaffe 1972)
3   (Bruce Bielaski, *Justice Aide*, Dies 1964)
4   (Bielaski 1917)
5   (S. A. Trone Business Agent, International General Electric Schenectady, N.Y. - suspected Radical, Testimony of Minorsky, D. F. Broderick September 11, 1920)
6   (S. Trone, State Department Solomon Trone Interview 1933) .
7   (Goldman, What I Believe 1908)
8   (Goldman, Address to the Jury by Emma Goldman, Delivered during her Anti-Conscription trial, New York City, July 9, 1917 1917)

9   (Jaffe 1972, 173)
10   (Big Bang on Wall Street 1920); (Havoc Wrought In Morgan Offices 1920)
11   (Perkins Defends Late J. P. Morgan 1915); (Iron Slugs Pierce Wall 1915); (Intruder Has Dynamite 1915); (Men Whose Lives Have Been Sought By Bomb Plotters 1919)
12   (Morgan 1971)
13   (Godine 1982, 157-158)
14   (Reich 1992); (Rothschild 2007)
15   (Chernow 2001); (J. P. Morgan, Jr. 1867-1943 1981)
16   (V. I. Lenin 1916)
17   (J. P. Morgan, Jr. 1867-1943 1981)
18   (Loth 1958, 176)
19   (Godine 1982, 157-158)
20   (Seagrave 1985)
21   (Thomas 1856); (Seaburg and Paterson 1971)
22   (Smalley 1981) ; (J. P. Morgan, Jr. 1867-1943 1981)
23   (Godine 1982, 157); (Harvard University 1941)
24   (U.S. Census 1880)
25   (Yesterday's Weddings 1892); (Married 1896); (Savage - Oudin 1926); (Obituary Notice 1928); (Mrs. Oudin Obituary 1956)
26   (Steinmetz August 1916)
27   (Trone, et al. 2009)
28   (Department of State 1916); (Godine 1982, 157-158); (Trone, et al. 2009); (Department of State 1917); (Federal Bureau of Investigations 1917-1921); (Weyl 2003)
29   (Trone, et al. 2009)
30   (Musk 1961)
31   (Canadian Immigration Agent Inspection 1917); (Passenger Manifest: Empress of Russia 1917)
32   (Godine 1982, 157-158)
33   (Johnston September 1905); (Meyer 1904, 121-140)
34   (Relief Goes To Siberia 1916)
35   (Trone, et al. 2009)
36   (Federal Bureau of Investigations November 9, 1917 – November 7, 1920); (Trone, et al. 2009); (General Electric 1925)
37   (Federal Bureau of Investigations November 9, 1917 – November 7, 1920); (S. Trone, Brief Outline of my Engineering Experience 1949); (S. Trone, Brief Sketch July 26, 1950); (S. Trone, Statement August 14, 1953); (Roth January 27, 1951, 83); (Mr. Trone Arriving in August 1949); (Trone, et al. 2009)
38   (Federal Bureau of Investigations November 9, 1917 – November 7, 1920)
39   (Godine 1982, 157-158)
40   (Godine 1982, 157-158)
41   (Federal Bureau of Investigations November 9, 1917 – November 7, 1920); (S. Trone, Brief Outline of my Engineering Experience 1949); (S. Trone, Brief Sketch July 26, 1950); (S. Trone, Statement August 14, 1953); (Roth January 27, 1951); (Mr. Trone Arriving in August 1949); (Trone, et al. 2009), (London, 2007); (Godine 1982, 157-158)
42   (Federal Bureau of Investigations November 9, 1917 – November 7, 1920)
43   (Canadian Immigration Agent Inspection 1917); (Passenger Manifest: Empress of Russia 1917); (Weyl 2003); (Federal Bureau of Investigations November 9, 1917 – November 7, 1920)
44   (Fawcett 2000, 68)
45   (Fawcett 2000, 68)
46   (Canadian Immigration Agent Inspection 1917); (Weyl 2003); (Federal Bureau of Investigations November 9, 1917 – November 7, 1920)
47   (Weyl 2003)
48   (Department of State 1917)

Chapter 2

THE WORLD OF TOMORROW

The Errand Boy and the Emperor

On the trip into Russia, the affable but diplomatic pair of Oudin and Waterman would not have been much conversation companions to Perkins. Perkins however loved nothing more than to debate and while not showing a great deal of erudition in his arguments he was extremely forthright in the language he used[1]. Perkins was smart, straight to the point and loved to win an argument. Whether debating arcane points of law in the courtroom or knotty philosophical principles in the lecture halls of his beloved Harvard, Perkins lived to debate.

It is for this reason more than any other that Trone was the essential traveling companion to Perkins when going in and out of Russia in 1916-1917. Trone was full of wit, and brimming with a detailed knowledge of the world, Perkins would argue from philosophical first principles and never give an inch. Important of course would be the cause for debate, something they had in large amounts. Trone was the arch-radical wanting to tear the old order out root and branch, while Perkins was the defender of the established elite and argued for the preservation of the old order.

The debate raged on a round trip from New York, across the entire lengths of the two biggest countries in the world, Canada and Russia, and across the longest ocean trip in the world, across the Pacific. This was a match made in heaven for the both of them, both tireless and keen to continue their debate, while a polite audience of Waterman and Oudin sat and watched the show. Neither Trone nor Perkins would have felt the loss of Waterman and Oudin for the journey back to New York, so enjoyable were their debates[2].

Perkins appreciated the opportunity of debate provided by Solomon Trone so much that he cabled his wife in Petrograd to send a copy of the Perkins family history to Trone's New York address as a gift. It was a rare and special moment for Perkins to find someone who could equal him in debate. Perkins did his work well but his greatest happiness in life did not come from what he saw as running "errands" for his corporate masters, particularly J. P. Morgan Jr. [3].

When Thomas Nelson Perkins gave his advice, so it was said, it was "... hard-headed common sense, often expressed in a picturesque vernacular"[4]. This meant that, among other things, his colourful language filled with expletives was not the type to be used in polite company. As one commentator put it, "he expressed himself with unforgettable phrases[5]." Many times his listeners would stand with their mouths open giving him rapt attention, merely because they could not believe what they were hearing and how they were hearing it said. Perkins' open and even blunt manner appealed to the powerful men he dealt with throughout his life. Perkins cultivated an image of physical toughness and rectitude. It was the business of Perkins to be blunt, to tell difficult, complicated and often unwanted truths in a clear and simple manner to men in positions of great power.

His obituary would describe him as "Descended from one of the foremost families of New England" and "...universally popular in his youth, captain of a famous Harvard Crew in 1891...[6]" Without a doubt, Perkins had been born into a very privileged world. This combined with his exceptional physical condition and love of sports gave him the reputation of tough a hard headed captain of industry who talked straight and made the deals. In his career he brokered some of the most critical agreements in the early part of the twentieth century not only for Morgan's financial interests but also for the United States, its allies and even its enemies.

Perkins was also a director for some of the most important the financial interests and corporations[7]. As his note to his passport application reads in 1916 he went to Petrograd to not only represent the interests of General Electric but also the interests of the American International Corporation (A.I.C.)[8]. The A.I.C. was a central financing corporation that united and directed an associated collection of important industrial and financial corporations[9].

When Trone and Perkins arrived back at the New York Grand Central Station in May of 1917 their first objective after visiting the GE headquarters in Schenectady would have been to meet with J. P. Morgan Jr. face to face. He was the only person who could answer what had been offered by the new Russian government in power. Morgan it appears held the ultimate power in the set of financial interests needed to create such a broad agreement.

The location for that meeting would have been Morgan's 219 Madison Avenue, Brownstone Mansion. It is one of the more august and palatial houses in all of New York City. In style its interior is barely indistinguishable from that of the banking family palaces of the Italian Renaissance. Like a modern day Borgia, Morgan wanted his power to be manifest in the high culture of priceless art. Now a museum and library, the Brownstone Mansion on Manhattan Island in New York City was in 1917 the center of Morgan's empire.

Both parties were not yet at the stage of writing the contract for the secret agreement. Perkins, holding a doctorate of law and having had years of experience in legal practice would have been more than capable of that task. What was required was something more than a contract, what was needed was a plan so grand it would literally re-write the rule book on the way the world's industry and business operated. The plan would go well beyond the world of a Harvard legal professor and East Coast aristocrat like Perkins.

Despite Perkins' own earthiness in the way he conducted negotiations, what was needed was someone even earthier, that person was Gerard Swope. As we will see Swope was so earthy he required a second person to act as a front-man for him when dealing with other human beings socially other than his family. By comparison Perkins was practically genteel and charming in negotiations.

We do not know exactly what must have happened in the meetings that occurred after Trone and Perkins arrived back in New York, or what eventual reports would have been given to Morgan in his study at the Brownstone Mansion.

What we do know is that there was some secret agreement between the Morgan's financial interests and the Russian Revolutionaries[10]. Not only do we find continuing relations with the Provisional and then Bolshevik government in Trone's files in the St. Petersburg historical archive but this confirms Trone's own autobiographical statements that he continued to work in Russia for General Electric helping the government of the day continuously well into the late 1920s[11].

Up to this point in 1917 American corporations were all about accumulating what already existed. The industries, the steel mills, the railroads and even the banks of the United States had been taken over and accumulated by owners of capital such as J. P. Morgan Junior.

This massive force for accumulation had begun to reach the limits of their power. Their method of operating was by now well known. Merging industries, nationally and internationally, cornering the markets and conspiring to fix prices to their benefit and to their profit. The problem was one of scale; the world of their financial and industrial empire in the Americas was just too small. They needed a broader and deeper level of economic and political control, something had to change. As we will see that change could only occur with the triumph of a Global Revolution that changed the way the world did business.

The Making of Morgan

Originally the Morgan Banking family had begun as mere agents of the Rothschild Banking house in New York. This was a good start as it was probably in that service that the Morgans learned some of the most important elements of getting rich. By following the working life of Dr. Solomon Trone one can see numerous examples of how well Morgan learned those lessons and had found improvements.

The Rothschild Banking House had developed into their wealthy position thanks to their innovations and particularly their good luck out of someone else's bad luck. The main innovation was to maintain tight control over a wide network of agents. These agents fed information and resources throughout the network. As the principal agents were all close loyal family members this was not a difficulty.

Building a wide network of agents was something that Morgan understood, copied and improved upon. Morgan would create complex webs of inter-connecting organizations and individuals working multiple roles. These organizations fed information and resources throughout the network, often unaware of how interconnected and how hidden were the real purpose of their operations.

While Trone the revolutionary was being paid to negotiate with the Bolsheviks in Petrograd, Perkins the conservative was preparing with the State Department the invasion of U.S. soldiers to crush the Bolsheviks in Russia. Whether building the economic infrastructure of Soviet Russia or that of the Anti-Bolshevik Mussolini's Italy, Morgan's enterprises worked both sides at once. Whether in the First or the Second World War, Morgan had a wide network of agents and organizations across the globe, across battle lines and frontiers.

Trone in this sense was not an unusual member of Morgan's apparatus. Trone never had to hide his political views, it was not until after he had been arrested in the 1905 Revolution that Trone's career was promoted to that of Managing director. Morgan's trust was based upon loyalty and honesty within the network, but not shared ideology or political creed.

The great business advantage presented by having a wide, complex and loyal network of agents was not the only similarity shared by the Banking Houses of Rothschild and Morgan. Morgan also had the benefit of being ready to make the best of good luck when it occurred. Both organizations could turn their strategies completely around at a moment's notice, if necessary. Morgan however had the advantage of being able to create the situations that he would profit from. The Rothschild Banking House did nothing to create or even encourage the wars they profited from; Morgan however was not above giving historical forces a nudge in a direction that would advantage him.

Morgan's Banking House cultivated and courted revolutionaries such as Solomon Trone. When the Russian Revolution broke out, Trone was found to be helping the revolutionaries by Oudin. Trone was on the front lines of the street fighting throughout the various phases of the 1917 revolution. As a paid employee of Morgan, Trone was giving advice to the Bolsheviks continuously. Such support to push history in the direction it wanted would have been unthinkable and simply impossible for the Rothschild Banking House.

The world where the Rothschild family built their fortune was one radically different from the one that saw the rise of the House of Morgan. The early nineteenth century was seeing the dawn of global economics and global warfare, two elements central to Rothschild's success. While Morgan had control of banks, industries and to a certain extent governments, the Rothschild Banking House had a more limited role.

Trone, as an agent of Morgan's, was constantly moving between organizations that managed capital investments, engineering corporations and political movements. Rarely did Trone have a home in one country for more than several months at a time. To a large extent this was made possible by the innovations in transportation and communication in the twentieth century.

Back in the Nineteenth Century these innovations did not exist. The Rothschild Banking House was dependent on having its agents travel by sailing ships and horse drawn carriages. The control of the economy by the Rothschild Banking house was also limited to the money and gold it could lend whereas Morgan would have a near total monopoly on the industries that his loans financed. The difference between the Rothschild and Morgan Banking houses was both in scale and in variety. Rothschild's world was much simpler and easier to understand.

In the age of the Rothschilds, the ongoing wars between Britain and France were mostly decided by their ability to finance loans to continue the fighting. Principally it was the access to gold reserves that proved critical as this was necessary to raise vast armies and navies to do battle globally. Access to gold reserves was exactly what the Rothschild Banking House had. They could get gold from the supposedly closed Napoleonic Europe and lend it to the Anti-Napoleon government of Britain across the English Channel. This was the advantage pure and simple of the Rothschild banking House.

The Rothschild Banking House owned the restaurant where the British and the French met to consume the world. The more their appetite for fighting the wealthier became the Rothschild Banking House. Rothschild did not create or direct the appetite of those it served. Personally the Rothschild family members found the actions of the French and British governments inexplicable. When the whole mess, called the Napoleonic Wars, was over they hoped through the exercise of their power to withhold capital to prevent such a global conflagration ever happening again.

Pacifism was a sentiment that Morgan never professed and of him could never be accused. Morgan's agents worked to create conflict, as conflict by its very nature fed Morgan's profits. Agents like Trone would help communist revolution world wide while pro-fascist agents as we will see later such as Thomas Lamont promoted, funded and advised governments who were dedicated to crushing Communism world wide. This cultivated the conditions for further conflict between political groups for supremacy. Morgan, if anything, was an enemy to Peace. Trone, as a revolutionary, was not an anomaly to Morgan's organization; he was an integral part of it.

It is true of course that despite their pacifist beliefs the Rothschild's did, just like Morgan, make a tidy profit from lending money to increasingly reckless debt ridden empires intent of murdering each other. As a family, thanks to these profits, they had gone in a matter of a few decades from being an ostracized ethnic minority living in a ghetto, to being accepted and raised to the aristocracy by many of the royal houses of Europe. The Rothschilds were complicit to the operations of the powerful in particular in their wars. Morgan however had gone way beyond mere complicity to war associated with the Rothschild banking house; Morgan promoted it.

It is clear that the Morgan Banking House learned the lesson of the Rothschild's success and then some. The Morgan's used their organizational abilities and advanced technology of the day to build a broad network of control that defied not only conventional business wisdom of the time but it also defied the control of the United States government.

Since the early revolutionary days of the United States there was a distrust of corporations enshrined in its legal foundations that set the rules for how its government and markets worked. A central bank and many of the other government institutions that are necessary for large corporations to operate legally did not exist.

The simple reason was that the American Revolution or alternatively called War of Independence was largely about overthrowing the large corporations that had been imposed on their country by their imperial overlords in London. These corporations owned the land, monopolized the trade and made life for the peasant immigrant particularly difficult. These corporations were seen as merely stripping the wealth of the country and sending it to the absentee owners across the ocean living a decadent lifestyle on their palatial estates in the English countryside.

After the revolution the liberated Americans made sure that a constitution when it was eventually written did not allow for big corporations to exist outside of their control. The key to Morgan's success was finding a way out of that control, so he could establish his network of power. To do this Morgan in the face of government and popular opposition monopolized industries, established a central bank and profited handsomely from America's internal and external military conflicts. J. P. Morgan Jr.'s ideology was summed up in his remarkably open statement of principle, "A certain number of men owning property should do what they like with it, and act in harmony."

Morgan and his agents such as Trone wanted to create through mergers and acquisitions a "community-of-interest plan." This plan would control the entire global economy. Creating a plan for the industrial control of society was Morgan's ultimate aim. Unlike the passive Rothschild Banking House that looked for opportunities, Morgan made his opportunities. Morgan actively promoted his vision of the world through enormous planning structures that encompassed numerous corporations.

Dr. Solomon Trone was considered a planning expert not because he was associated with the Bolsheviks and their Five Year Plans, but because he was an agent of Morgan. From the start of his career to the end of his life, Trone worked tirelessly to create large scale industrial plans that were designed to create a harmonious community of needs, hopes, efforts, resources and interests.

To create such enormous plans Morgan needed to own and accumulate more and more. To be sure, Morgan owned an enormous amount of industries and corporations. Everyone knew it, and the government had already tried and failed to take it away. The anti-trust acts meant to break Morgan's banking, railroad, steel and electrical industry monopolies were woefully inadequate to catch Morgan. Unlike Rockefeller's oil monopoly Morgan had effectively and entirely insulated his holdings from the prying eyes of the U.S. federal authorities. If the business of America is Business, then mostly what America did was Morgan's business.

Within the space of a few generations the Morgan Banking Family had gone from being an agent of the European banking houses to being the effective power in the land; one that kept the federal government from bankruptcy, ran the railroads, had the national industries dependent on his steel and those industries were largely powered by the electricity of his corporations generated.

The problem if there was one came from his competition with Europe. Specifically the problem was linked to colonies. As much as he might be the power in the land of America, the rest of the world was divided up by the colonial powers of Europe. Morgan's attempts to acquire more European holdings had been stymied by political controls he could not buy off.

When the Parliament in Britain, at the behest of its capitalists, stopped Morgan from taking over their public transportation system in London, he was flabbergasted. He called it "the greatest rascality and conspiracy I ever heard of." Praise indeed from Morgan.

He could not join them, and he had not yet found a way to beat them. Entire continents were controlled by European monarchies and effectively shut to him. Unless imperial Europe collapsed and collapsed utterly, his dreams of being a truly global power were only dreams. Dreams of destroying the European monarchies and their control of colonies were shared however by at least one of his employees, the revolutionary Dr. Solomon Trone.

In 1917 the news that one of his debtors, Russia, was now bankrupt and had been taken over by new Revolutionary owners must have made Morgan sit up and take notice. It was always sad to lose an investment but it was not all bad news. In the collapse there was some glimmering of future Capitalist happiness that Morgan even in that moment could discern.

The relevant news was brought back by the unlikely combination of the tall svelte rough talking Aristocrat Perkins and the small squat smooth talking Russian Revolutionary Trone. The news of the Revolutionary opportunities gave Morgan a hint his dream of global dominance was about to be realized.

Morgan was on the verge of reaping the benefits of a well organized network of control thanks to an incredible stroke of good luck. Good luck it should be noted that was the direct result of some else's incredible bad luck.

The News from Nowhere

When the First World War had seemed inevitable banking interests such as J. P. Morgan Jr. took precise precautions to make sure he could profit from both sides[12]. He told the U.S. State Department he owned property and had money lent out to the enemy. The State Department appears not to have had a problem with this as no action was taken. Considering his man Perkins was in large measure running important work for the State Department at the time it is little wonder such a confession elicited such a strange benediction[13].

To really profit from the conflict though capitalists needed their operations to be close to the action, but safe from being plundered while maintaining control of their interests on both sides of the battlefield. In particular he needed to transfer their assets to a neutral place close by both of the main combatants so they could operate their armament factories and lend money to both sides. To be able to do this they needed men of proved ability, loyalty and discretion to go on a quick errand to Switzerland. Such employees for General Electric and Morgan's other financial interests who would make that trip early years of the war to Zurich were Gerard Swope and his close associate and lieutenant Clark Haynes Minor[14].

While Minor would later talk quite openly about the activities with Swope and Trone, his own activities he was sure to cover in some obscurity. Being discrete, Minor would ask for and get to keep his expired passport that covered the period of WWI. This was not to cover any evidence of travels of course, but merely for "sentimental reasons"[15].

Swope, on the other hand, did not appear to be so subtle. Playing true to his rather rough and myopic character, did not know that he may be accused of treason, or at the very least of profiteering from the war. In fact Swope did not even know there was a war[16]. When he did find out there was a war on, he accidently found out about it at the race track. He was looking through the newspaper trying to figure out which horse to place a bet on. He was also quite unaware of who was fighting or why they were fighting until much later. Luckily for him, these were details he did not have to know, he just had to follow orders. As the European armies were mobilizing to devastate their civilization and sacrifice a generation to a senseless death, Swope shrugged and said the situation, "hardly warranted the fuss."

The transfer of Morgan's European corporate bases to a neutral and accessible location required that agents such as Trone, Minor and Swope arrive in the Swiss financial capital, Zurich, in the fall of 1914. It is interesting to note that in the exact same week as Morgan was relocating his European headquarters to Zurich, the Russian Vladimir Lenin was also relocating the exiled community of his Bolshevik party to Zurich as well.

Three years later, all the hard work of American financiers to profit from the war had incurred the opposite effect. Instead of a return on investment they were now looking at the ruin of their wealth. The advanced military technology of the time that American business was largely responsible for selling at a high profit margin was ideal for defensive warfare only. Every advance was costly, and to advance too far into the enemy lines meant risking the decimation of your entire army. Even if an army did make advances, these advances could not be held and were always pushed back in counter attacks.

It must have been clear to Morgan by 1917 that Trone and his fellow engineers had been too successful in modernizing the military infrastructure of Europe. The electrification and mechanization of transportation, communication and military production, all made possible through Morgan corporations and capital loans, had made the nation states of Europe virtually impregnable to defeat and powerless to attain victory. All the war had achieved were staggering depletions of men, machines and capital. Before long no one would be able to pay anything back to anybody. The great arrogant European powers and their advanced technology had engineered its own destruction at the very height of their power.

Morgan must have been livid. What had seemed a sure bet, for making money hand over fist, had brought him to a situation where each passing day meant incalculable losses. Each combatant nation he had bet on needed more weapons from his industries, more capital from his banks and most of all they all needed more time to pay.

If war was a disappointment to Morgan, peace loomed like an absolute disaster. Someone must pay for all this bloodshed and horror, and Morgan was determined that it would not be him. If the war continued and bankrupted everyone, bringing down governments and with it establishing peace there would be no victory and no plunder from the loser to pay the financial interests that owned the debt. Morgan was in a bind, and just as his agents had got him into this situation, Trone and Perkins now offered him a way out.

Of course what had happened in Russia must have put the fright into Morgan like nothing else could. The soldiers no longer wished to fight, and in Russia they had put their sentiment into action deserting the front lines and overthrowing their government. The Russian soldiers were not alone; German, British and French soldiers had the same sentiment to mutiny and in some cases had even acted on it. A declaration of universal peace without victory and its accompanying pillage of the loser would have been the ruin of the investors who had made the loans to the combatant nations.

What Morgan wanted now was another way out, a third option to either peace or war. That option came unexpectedly from none other than the anti-Capitalist Bolshevik leader Vladimir Lenin.

Although we do not know exactly how the deal was brokered, Trone and Perkins must have made it abundantly clear to the Russian government that the boss back in New York wanted his money. It did not matter what type of persons were the new managers of Russia, to Morgan, the money owed was still outstanding. It is for this reason that the new government had to come up with some novel ways to pay the bills. It was probably at this moment back in Petrograd when Trone and Perkins confronted them with the idea of rebuilding Russia based upon a colossal plan, using J. P. Morgan Jr.'s corporations. In essence it was to forget the debt created before and during the war by the previous owner the Czar, and in turn Russia's new rulers would agree to a bigger deal and a much bigger debt to American capital.

In essence this was an effort to come up with an alternative method of payment, the new government was in effect refinancing their loans with the banks. The previous method of payment was to continuing the fighting until the Allies had the opportunity to plunder Germany for the debt they owed. This was clearly not working. Russia by the end of 1917 had lost eight and a quarter million people in death and casualties. Tens of millions of young men on all sides had been bayoneted, shelled, gassed, and machine gunned. Each side had become locked into positions that had scarcely moved since the first months of the war.

Far from the glorious dreams of victory within a matter of weeks and months, to the surprise of all, the war had proved a contest where victory was impossible and destruction inevitable. Trone who designed and directed the electrification of Russia's military installations must have been well aware of how futile warfare had become by 1917. The slaughter had become a monument to the power of modern engineering.

The deal the new government would offer to Morgan could not be agreed to by Perkins. For Perkins this was too big a deal and too dangerous to be negotiated by him. He could of course proceed back to New York City, with Trone, and give in person to J. P. Morgan Jr. the deal that was being offered. This was an errand that Perkins could do and did.

The days when the Perkins family of Boston, the great East Coast Mandarins could act on their own was over. They were no longer the independent operators they were when they traded in drugs and slaves, or owned the railroads. The family and its assets had been subsumed into something much bigger; a vast global organization that we may call Morgan's financial interests. And this particular Perkins, Thomas Nelson Perkins, ran the most important errands for this set of interests.

The deals of the Perkins family in the Nineteenth Century were not in the same league as the deals of the Morgan family in the Twentieth. Thomas Perkins had realized this long ago and made the best of the situation. Although he was a loyal servant of Morgan, his real passion was for Harvard University and the advancement of scholarly learning. He gave so much of his time to the University that they named a building after him there when he died, and it took a decade for them to cease lamenting in print about his death. Harvard was his true love and one that loved him back just as intensely.

Thomas Perkins said later in life that, "When I got out of law school, I went to work for a law firm (that represented the Morgan financial interests) and began running errands. I have been running other people's errands ever since[17]." The latest generation in the Perkins family had produced the errand boy for the interests of big business. He was massively educated, had an aristocratic pedigree that could be traced directly to Charlemagne and the noble houses of Europe, but he was in essence Morgan's man for running errands around the globe.

When Perkins and his coworker Trone had come to Petrograd to collect the bill owed to J. P. Morgan Jr. they found that there were new and very different people in charge in Russia. These new people had very novel ideas, ideas that were not only strange and new but they also made sense and seemed profitable. These people were responsive to a large scale planning approach to industry; to them such grand scale planned economic development was their highest political objective.

Trone of course knew these people and their objectives as these were many of the same political comrades that he had been arrested with in 1905. Trone knew personally many who were in positions of authority in the new Provisional Government[18]. Some of these were electrical engineers just like Trone. He knew that men such as these would have shared objectives with the interests of American corporations, because he shared those objectives. It was a common element throughout the various political groups that now controlled Russia; Russia must be modernized on a grand scale. Russia was backward, and suffered because of her backwardness.

Trone did not expect to find his former comrades in control of what was the Russian Empire, but on finding them there he seems not to have wasted a minute in promoting an agreement with the American business and financial interests that would rebuild Russia. As we shall see later, not all of Trone's comrades were in agreement with each other, but enough were at this point to make a proposal of sorts, unofficial perhaps, possible.

Lenin in his book on the *Latest Stage of Imperialism* had done extraordinarily deep research into the contemporary wealth of nations. He had researched the relationship between big money, and the newly emerging electrical industry, in respect to which nations were powerful and which were not. In particular He looked at the successes of Sweden and showed how its advanced electrical industry led to its present position among the wealthier nations.

Lenin's Bolsheviks were politically, economically and technically savvy. Most of all however they were not the Russian political radicals of old, whose great esoteric morality, deep convictions and commitments to sacrifice alienated them from Western European sensibilities. These men talked the language of global big business and contemporary technology.

As rare as it may seem to find Russian political radicals who could talk business, Morgan had something equally rare to match; American businessmen who could talk radical politics. Morgan's men were not all from elite society; some of them read the great anarchist authors of the Nineteenth Century and spent their off hours debating the ways and means to bring about a new world order. The foremost and the most important of these men was Gerard Swope. He was a revolutionary who meant business, and knew how to make the business of revolution profitable.

For Love and Revolution

The last journal entry in 1917 that we have for Henrietta Swope, the daughter of Gerard Swope, is dated Oct. 27, and concerns a visit to a Shinto temple in Japan. Her entry on the previous day tells of a boat ride on which she and her father and brother "had a little rough house to make the time go faster[19]." Gerard Swope loved to do physical activity with his children. He loved horseback riding with them and his favor ite activity was wrestling and this is how he spent his last days before he and his wife and children took a train apparently to see a Russia in the midst of radical change.

Swope was a busy man of limited intellectual breadth outside of what was required for managing General Electric. He loved his kids very dearly but as his authorized biography readily admits, he was perhaps not the ideal of fatherhood. He was not the kind of man who loved to spend time talking or just being social. He loved to calculate and he loved to control[20].

We know he respected Solomon Trone, precisely because he was a man of ability and intelligence. As with all his employees, Gerard Swope judged men by a limited criterion, did they have the intelligence and ability to do what he wanted? On both points Trone fit the bill adequately. For this reason it can reasonably be presumed Gerard would deputize Solomon Trone and his son Dmitri Trone to execute his and GE's plans for Russia[21].

Many people who knew Swope thought he was a born manager, and certainly Gerard Swope never had any doubts. At an early age Gerard Swope began his managerial career. That age was twelve. Of course at the time he only had one person to boss around and that was his younger brother. There is nothing unusual in this of course, except the manner of it. Gerard Swope insisted and got reports each week from his brother detailing specified sets of activities and objectives that he had accomplished during the week. A little later on, his brother had to send an income and expense report to his brother at regular intervals also[22].

Throughout Gerard Swope's life he only had one imperative, to make all the lines of authority lead to him. His motto, which he repeated as often as he could was, "analyze, organize, deputize, and supervise"[23]. The last of these was not an idle operation for Gerard Swope, his capacity and love of detail made it a point of honour to know often as much as his subordinates about their work. As one of his closest colleagues was to say, "In all my years with the General Electric Company, Swope never gave anyone a freehand. He was the directing boss[24]."

When he was put in charge of General Electric as a co-President with Owen D. Young, he made it quite clear that he would "do all the work"[25]. All Owen had to do was be the public persona of the corporation. Of course this apparent lack of vanity was really due to a serious social failure. Swope's inability to relate to people was legendary.

Starting at the meager salary of a dollar a day on G.E.'s shop floor, he felt no sense that his pride was wounded. His M.I.T. education, he felt, did not entitle him to a nice office. He wanted more than anything else to understand the technology. His love of machines had driven him to get the education of an engineer and then go and work as a technician on the shop floor of a GE factory. He wanted to understand the machines from the ground up. He related not to the organization first but to its products. Nothing gave Swope more satisfaction out of life than perfect running machines and well organized operations that would use the machines. An absolute efficiency of purpose, design and execution was the ideal of Swope[26].

Swope was valuable to GE, despite the fact he was not fit often for the polite company of other human beings. Early in Swope's career a manager had given him a Latin phrase that he should repeat over and over again, "suaviter in modo, fortiter in re" (gently in manner, strongly in deed). Of course Swope would remain Swope, regardless of whatever Latin phrases GE made him repeat over and over again like a naughty schoolboy[27].

For Solomon Trone, who was not such a good engineer and was extremely social, his relationship with Gerard Swope was built upon a shared interest in something one would not expect; political movements to promote social justice. A letter exists where Trone, in later life, wrote to Swope telling him how he has travelled the world looking into social questions such as the "causes of unrest"[28]. He asks Swope to help him further his humanitarian activities. Swope responds by helping Trone get positions in the government and in charitable organizations exactly so he can do just that[29].

As direct and cold as Gerard Swope could be, there was another side to him that seems almost inexplicable, that was his humanitarian political interests. It is an element that is entirely at odds with his rather unsocial character. To understand where this element came from you have to know the woman who more than anyone else made Gerard Swope the man he was.

It has been said that behind every great man there is a woman. Sexist though the phrase maybe, with Gerard Swope there was more than a little truth to this statement. The woman he married required an odd courtship, one that had Gerard sitting through lectures by Anarchists like Kropotkin and volunteering in the poorest neighborhoods in Chicago giving free lessons in mathematics to anyone who needed it. She made him work for her love, and as Gerard Swope embraced the challenge his love for her grew. Unlike Solomon Trone who had numerous lovers throughout his life, often simultaneously, Gerard was a "one-woman-man." That woman however had to be demanding and her love must be difficult if not seemingly impossible to obtain. His overwhelming sense of pride in his abilities would demand no less. That woman was Henrietta Hill. Their meeting was entirely due to chance and the radical politics of Chicago at that time[30].

When Gerard Swope was transferred to Chicago he ran into an old school friend. That old school friend, so Gerard Swope says, was involved in the operations of a place that offered social services on a chartable basis. It was called Hull House. Swope had nothing to do in this new city where he had arrived. He knew few people and did not have any hobbies outside of work. He was a man who hated having nothing to do, so he helped his friend offering to volunteer at Hull House.

Hull House in Chicago is where the center of political dissent in the city coalesced at the time. As Gerard Swope became involved in its operations, he was coming face to face with one of the greatest and most influential radical social and political experiments in the world.

Founded in 1889 Hull House grew to a complex of thirteen buildings, including a theater, art gallery, clubs, dining hall, nursery school, residence for working women, the only library in the neighborhood, and one of the first free gymnasiums in the country. More than a thousand people from the neighborhood came to the settlement each week for its education, artistic, and social programs.

The members of Hull House, mostly women, pushed for social reforms. Their triumphs were stunning. They established the world's first juvenile court, the city's first public playground, and they campaigned for improved housing regulations, sanitation, public schools, and entered vigorously into local politics. Among the initiatives they which promoted were pensions for women, occupational health and safety regulations, child labor laws, and perhaps most successfully woman's suffrage.

Hull House was built by Jane Addams the socialist, feminist, anti-war, pacifist, and uncompromising radical. Campaigns by the rich and the powerful of Chicago to "Get Rid of Jane" would follow her throughout her life, but she would not budge from her radical ideology. From a privileged back ground, she was ostracized from the elite community she had grown up in, as a traitor. Later in Jane's life she was honoured as one of the United States' most influential and important citizens, wining recognition internationally when she was given the Nobel Prize for peace. Some of course would still be cursing her as a "dangerous woman" even when she was in her eighties.

Jane inspired many women from different social and political groups to join with her in struggle. It is directly from Jane's female disciples that we will see some of Trone's closest allies the Swope's and his fiercest enemy. Jane inspired the one person who we will see later who would achieve what the FBI, the Gestapo and the Soviet state security forces could not, Trone's defeat ending of his career.

Jane's development of the "Hull House Settlement" inspired a generation of feminists and social activists who would eventually remake America and to a large extent the world. Jane's agenda was not just to deal with the symptoms of social inequality, such as extreme poverty and prejudice, but to attack the causes of the disease. Women's rights, such as the right to be independent of the control of husbands and fathers, and the right of women to engage in politics were the essential foundations of her ideology.

Jane's broad feminist ideology united women of across social and economic divisions. It is not surprising therefore that her Hull House ideology attracted the attention and admiration of Henrietta Hill. She was from both a privileged and a radical background. She was heiress to one of the great radical traditions of the United States because her father was one of the foremost Liberals in America[31].

Henrietta's ancestors were forced to emigrate out of England almost a century before because of radical egalitarian religious principles. Her parents were highly educated, political radicals to whom the epithet of unorthodox would not be amiss. Her father Thomas Hill had many different careers, had an enduring love of science, published many political works, and was an ardent abolitionist. As well as campaigning against slavery Thomas Hill was also the President of Harvard, during the Civil War.

In a word the Hills were American Liberals. Trone commented about this particular and unusual section of American society when he said, "Occasionally you find here representatives of a special human breed-American: liberals. Gentlemen, our radical intellectuals are good and honest. It would be foolish to think that America is all standardized and that it consists only of dollar-chasing, only of bridge games or poker[32]." The Hills stood for high moral principles, the perfectibility of the human spirit, the individualism of Thoreau, Emerson and Whitman, dedication to serve the poorest of the poor and most of all they stood for the rational liberation of the mind.

The Hills may have stood apart from the majority of American society, but they were culturally very American. They conformed to the overriding professed standard of America, efficiency. As Trone put it, "Americans know how to be carried away by ideals. And since in general they are business people and know how to work, they are just as efficient in the revolutionary movement, when they also attend to business and not to a lot of talk[33]." This was the Hills all over, radical and they were dedicated with an efficiency that was breath taking.

Her efficiency, dedication to hard work and her uncompromising ideology, not to mention her tallness in comparison to Swope and good looks, made her the romantic challenge that became the central focus of and perhaps the single most important aspect of Swope's life. She was the woman who would give him his ideological principles, the woman who he would give up his Jewish religion for; she was the woman who would give him his single greatest idea in the whole of his professional career.

It took many months from his meeting her at Hull House before she would agree to meet with him socially. When they did meet it was on her terms. They would go to the countryside on a tandem bicycle. Gerard would do all the cycling while his love sat on the seat in front steering and giving him lectures on progressive economic policy and political ideology. Up hills and down, Gerard appears to have learned from Henrietta something of her radical and liberal views. Perhaps the single most important lesson was planning; life must develop into something better. Just as the settlement movement saw community development as fundamental. It is not in getting power that makes life better; by itself power serves no purpose. Power must have a purpose.

Like the love of a mother there is power in bringing something new into the world; the power to bring a child into the world and raise it to take part in the life of the community. Bringing a theoretical future into existence through planning was exactly what Trone would travel the world endlessly selling; selling the world of tomorrow.

It is the introduction of Henrietta into the life of Gerard that a new element was implanted into the community-of-interest plans of the financial interests of Morgan. It all occurred when Gerard Swope was sent on a business trip to Texas. After that trip, nothing on earth would be quite the same again.

Straight from Hull House, where development was the key to everything, Gerard Swope went into a room full of Texas and Mexican businessman and local municipal officials. It was a not a prosperous community they represented, but they wanted it to be. Because of this they had a problem. They needed money to buy massive electrical generators to run an industrial base they hoped to eventually build. The problem was that without an industrial base, the community was too poor to pay for the massive electrical generators. At this time such purchases were not made on credit but up front before the generators were delivered.

The dilemma down in Texas was presented to Gerard Swope as an unsolvable conundrum. He was sent there as a last ditch effort to see if a deal could be reached that worked in Morgan's interest. It was at this moment Gerard Swope thought up a plan that sent him dashing across the border, on his own initiative to see some business men in Mexico City. What he was looking for was not merely to find more business men to join in the project; he was looking for something much deeper much more important. He had an idea and he need time to develop it[34].

When he emerged from Mexico, he came back with plans and figures that were as novel as they were prescient of what industry would become. He wanted Morgan to sell something that was much more than mere electrical generators. He would sell plans for future industrial development directly to the community on credit, without any middle men, and the machines were only an incidental part of the deal. The plan would include machines, but it would include much more, it would include the implicit development of factories, housing, social infrastructure, schools, and large scale industrialized farming. The plan if realized would lock the community into buying not just electrical generators, but factories, tractors and housing; they would be buying the development of their community, they would be buying the world of tomorrow.

Executives were not pleased to hear what Gerard Swope was saying and they turned him down flat. It was radical, it was dangerous, and it just might work. This new way of planning, one that incorporated long term development, before they were paid for their investment would mean an entirely new way of doing business. This way of doing business required large scale cooperation with governments and the commitment of entire communities. This new way of doing business tied the American corporations to the communities to whom it sold its products.

Swope's radical idea was shelved, but it was not forgotten. Gerard Swope never forgot or forgave the insult to his genius and initiative. In the fateful spring of 1917, Gerard Swope's plan was brought forward, and Gerard Swope was sent on a mission to test his great idea.

As we will see in the spring and summer of 1917 Russia was also not quite ready for Swope's great experiment. Swope had to wait while some of Trone's most dedicated political comrades such as Leon Trotsky prepared the way.

Gerard Swope had left in April of 1917 to make his way to Petrograd by July of 1917[35]. Swope had planned to make a stop in Japan to do some business and then no doubt to wait in Harbin China for the word from Petrograd.

The political changes Gerard Swope seems to have expected in July did not happen. Lenin's Bolsheviks attempted a coup and failed. Gerard, one can imagine was disheartened somewhat, but still hopeful as he telegrammed for his wife and children to join him waiting in China. Henrietta arrived at the end of the summer with their daughter, the future astronomer, Henrietta Swope and their son Isaac Swope. There they waited until it seemed as though the big event in Russia was never going to happen.

In September the Swopes' made their way to Japan. After sightseeing in China and enjoying the cultural attractions of Japan, Swope's daughter was having a great time. According to her diary which she wrote habitually almost each day, she was spending time enjoying conversing with her culturally sophisticated mother and wrestling and horseback riding with her father. Then suddenly on October 27 1917 the diary ends. The entire month around the Russian Revolution November 1917 was a blank[36].

The family seems to disappear off the face of the earth for one and half months. It is not until December the 10th 1917 that there is a record of the Swope family landing in Vancouver Canada. What happened between those two dates is something that would remain a secret with Swope saying that he had only spent that time in Japan and China[37].

What we know from Trone's file in the St. Petersburg Historical Archive is that a deal was reached by September 1917 that would be continuous through the Russian Revolution on November 7, 1917 into the period of the US military intervention in Russia in 1918[38]. Elsewhere we see the relationship with General Electric and the Soviet Union was continuous in the post war period until the recognition by the USA of the Soviet Union in 1934[39]. General Electric's relations with the Bolshevik government of Lenin were based on an agreement to industrialize and electrify what was the Russian Empire. That agreement would transform it from a backward society of illiterate peasants and agriculture to an educated population driving a modern industrial economy. It is clear that this agreement was reached before Lenin's party took power.

Endnotes

1   (Harvard University 1941, 9)
2   (Trone, et al. 2009)
3   (Business Historical Society November, 1937); (Trone, et al. 2009)
4   (Perkins Called "Leading Citizen of Country," Praised for His Devoted Service and Public Spirit by Fellow Officers 1937); (Harvard University 1941)
5   (Mr. T. N. Perkins An American's Public Service 1937)
6   (Mr. T. N. Perkins An American's Public Service 1937)
7   (Mr. T. N. Perkins An American's Public Service 1937); (Perkins Called "Leading Citizen of Country," Praised for His Devoted Service and Public Spirit by Fellow Officers 1937); (Harvard University 1941)
8   (Department of State 1916)
9   (Wikipedia 2011)
10   (S. Trone, General Electric Director's Records (Solomon Trone)Фонд 1367. Опись 8. Дело 1051 / Фонд 1367. Опись 8. Дело 1022 / ЦГИА. Фонд 1367. Опись 4. Дело 76 1916-1918)
11   (S. Trone, Brief Outline of my Engineering Experience 1949); (S. Trone, Brief Sketch July 26, 1950); (S. Trone, Statement August 14, 1953); (Roth January 27, 1951); (Mr. Trone Arriving in August 1949); (Trone, et al. 2009)
12   (Chernow 2001); (J. P. Morgan, Jr. 1867-1943 1981); (Frieden Winter, 1988); (Scheiber September 1969)
13   (Mr. T. N. Perkins An American's Public Service 1937); (Perkins Called "Leading Citizen of Country," Praised for His Devoted Service and Public Spirit by Fellow Officers 1937); (Harvard University 1941)
14   (Department of State 1915); (Loth 1958, 76); (SS Flandre 1914)
15   (Department of State 1918)
16   (Loth 1958, 76)
17   (Business Historical Society November, 1937)
18   (Trone, et al. 2009), (London, 2007); (Federal Bureau of Investigations November 9, 1917 – November 7, 1920); (S. Trone, Brief Outline of my Engineering Experience 1949); (S. Trone, Brief Sketch July 26, 1950); (S. Trone, Statement August 14, 1953); (Roth January 27, 1951)
19   (H. H. Swope 1917)
20   (Loth 1958, 113)
21   (D. Trone 1978)
22   (Loth 1958, 15-16)
23   (Loth 1958, 113)
24   (Loth 1958, 124)
25   (Loth 1958, 105)
26   (Loth 1958, 113)
27   (Loth 1958, 69)
28   (S. Trone, Correspondence from Trone to Swope 1939)
29   (G. Swope 1939)
30   (Loth 1958, 32-34)
31   (Harvard University Archives: Papers of Thomas Hill, biographical notes 2016)
32   (Ilf and Petrov 1937, 216)
33   (Ilf and Petrov 1937, 217)
34   (Loth 1958, 41-42)
35   (Department of State 1917)
36   (H. H. Swope 1917)
37   (G. Swope 1953)
38   (S. Trone, General Electric Director's Records (Solomon Trone)Фонд 1367. Опись 8. Дело 1051 / Фонд 1367. Опись 8. Дело 1022 / ЦГИА. Фонд 1367. Опись 4. Дело 76 1916-1918)
39   (Hoff 1974, 53)

Chapter 3

RUSSIAN ROULETTE

The Beautiful Loser

Trone was one of life's most beautiful losers. He lost at everything and yet continued on to the next adventure with the same optimism and enthusiasm as a small child discovering some new wonder in the world of the common place. Trone never gave up the joy he had for life, and never was fully able to be stopped by the immense tragedies that he witnessed firsthand. For him the great vision of the world that "could be" was overwhelming. When trying to say why his work had been important in the Soviet Union to the Writers Ilf and Petrov he was left speechless. "No, no, no! You cannot understand that!"[1]. He had seen something great and he would spend his entire life trying to translate this to mankind.

He was the direct descendent of a "wunderrabbi"; a miracle working rabbi. In myths wunderrabbi usually dispense curses and blessings and in the more extravagant tales performed exorcisms, broke the spells of witches and combated zombies. Of course a wunderrabbi was, in reality, most often a very wise and respected man who could advise a community what it should do in difficult situations, or successfully negotiate on behalf of the community with powerful lords and kings. The wunderrabbi was an exceptional combination of moral philosopher, teacher and political leader.

Trone however had many rabbis as his ancestors. His grandfather was a rabbi. His father was not. His father was secular and was a man who was fully modern in his approach to life. Solomon's upbringing was not very Jewish in either religion or culture; in fact he would not even speak Yiddish, the dialect of German common to the Jewish community at that time. Solomon was one of the middle children in a family of six. His father was a teacher and he tutored some of the children of the elite families in the Latvian area of the Russian Empire where they lived[2].

At a young age, possibly around twelve, Solomon Trone met a friend who would be a constant political comrade with him until he died. His name was Victor Podpali. Victor was the son of a school inspector who had traveled the Russian Empire grading how good the schools were. Out of all the schools for young boys in Russia Victor's father knew the best education was to be found in Latvia. They were the most modern because they most closely copied the German schools at that time[3].

While Victor and Solomon were in school together they were inspired by what they learned in their history lessons. They were galvanized by the teaching of history that was based upon the ideas of the German philosopher Friedrich Hegel. Much has been written about Hegelian philosophy and its effect on politics over the past century. It should be realized however that to Victor and Solomon their reading of Hegel was particular to who they were and where they were. Both were from families that looked to Germany as the place where culture and progress took place. The Germans had schools, libraries and universities open to everyone.

What Hegel said to the boys was that life flowed in the direction of becoming more and more like Germany. To a Russian in the nineteenth century this did not seem too bad at all. Hegel saw the height of civilization as the Germany he lived in. He saw all life as a progress to that particular place and time. Its not because Hegel said life is a force of progress always developing that inspired the young boys. To them he said, "I'm a German living a pretty good life and everyone can try to be just like me."

Solomon's family spoke German, throughout his life he would refuse to speak Yiddish. A quick look through his bookshelves at the time of his death shows that the language whose poetry and literature inspired him the most was German. It was particularly in Goethe and Rilke that he would return over and over again in his life[4].

It was not long before Trone and Podpali found underground Russian political literature. To them the stories of the clandestine political groups such as the Narodniks inspired them greatly. In particular, the life of Vera Figner inspired Trone. So much was Trone inspired he named his daughter after her.

Vera Figner had run a campaign of bombing and political intrigue during the late 1800s. She helped create the paramilitary wing of the political group, Narodnya Volya (People's Will). Thanks mainly to her dedication and skill this group managed to assassinate the Czar in 1881. She was intelligent and she had developed that intelligence through education in science in and philosophy in Switzerland. She was uncompromising and prepared to selflessly commit herself to the cause of liberating the Russian people.

Over the Nineteenth century Russia's political struggle for reform had undergone many twists and turns. At the end of the Nineteenth century Victor and Solomon would have benefited from what had become an extensive network of underground political groups and the clandestine literature they produced.

The reforming and radical movements of Russia had failed to bring progress. Life for peasants was as bad as it could be. In some cases life had become considerably worse. Nine out of ten Russians were still peasants, and now many of them were landless peasants. Where political reformers and radicals had failed to bring a real change to the lives of the people, they had succeeded in bringing about a real change in the lives of political people in Russia. They had produced the ideal of a political radical who was not only brave enough and strong enough to endure the hardships of political struggle but furthermore he was a sophisticate of learning and technical ability.

Stepniak was the Revolutionary who, for many, most embodied this ideal of dedication and intelligence. He would have been the most obvious inspiration for both Podpali and Trone in their teens in the 1890s. Why he would be the most obvious ideal for the revolutionary of the time, is a testament to Stepniak's skill in publishing and marketing as much as it is to his fighting ability as a political activist which were considerable.

Stepniak did not come from a wealthy background, but he was not desperately poor either. He went from getting a liberal education, a rarity at the time, to becoming an officer in the artillery. He learnt the methods of modern warfare as a professional soldier, these methods he would take to his work in politics. After a few arrests and escapes Stepniak would achieve a remarkable series of conquests. These triumphs would make nearly every one in Europe sit up and take notice. Certainly these events would have been of great importance to the young politically active Trone.

On the streets of Moscow Stepniak with only a knife as a weapon killed the head of the Czar's secret police. Escaping, Stepniak would then join others outside of the Russian Empire in helping to fight their struggles against oppression. In Bosnia Stepniak would help the insurgents in a desperate fight with the Ottoman Sultan. In Italy Stepniak would take to the hills in a heroic campaign with Anarchists to liberate the peasants.

In exchanging gunfire with the police Stepniak was fearless. As he liberated villages the sight of him and his fellow insurgents was a profound inspiration. Priests threw off their religious clothes and stamped on Christian icons and crosses while the peasants cheered and set fire to the police stations and government archives. It was as if Stepniak was bringing forth a new world, and everything associated with the peasants' oppression would be torched.

When finally captured in Italy Stepniak was prepared for his death. However in admiration for his bravery and the purity and justness of his cause, the Italian juries would not convict him. Much to Stepniak's great surprise when he was finally convicted by a judge, he was not executed but pardoned. What would have been death or at least a forced march in chains thousands of miles to Russia's Far East to a life of exile and hard labour, in Western Europe was brief prison stay and a pardon. Stepniak had found a world outside of Russia that was sympathetic to his cause. Stepniak was just the man to develop that sympathy into a force to help the Russian people.

Stepniak would make friends with such powerful literary allies as George Bernard Shaw and Mark Twain. Shaw would base his heroes on the character of Stepniak. Mark Twain would declare his absolute support for Russian political radicals and their more violent methods. After meeting Stepniak, Twain said, "If dynamiting each Czar in succession until no one wants the job of Czar is the only way to get rid of Czars – then God bless dynamite![5]"

Before long Stepniak was putting together his own publishing house for creating books that would encourage support for political change both inside and outside of Russia. The publishing house was so successful that some of his comrades would go on to success in the wider publishing world.

Perhaps the greatest most long lasting effect of Stepniak was his encouragement of a couple, Wilfred and Ethel Voynich. He introduced them to each other, encouraged them to take up publishing in order to help the political cause, and when he died his life was the source material for Ethel Voynich's powerful novel, "Gadfly." In the novel Stepniak's life, ideals and character is transformed into that of an Italian context. Out of a sense of deep grief for the loss of Stepniak, Ethel wrote a work so deeply compelling it was a best seller in Russia just before the Czar was overthrown. Because it was supposedly about an Italian, the official Russian censor did not realize that it was really about the feared Stepniak. Stepniak ideals and speeches exhorting political change were heard again, after his death, throughout Russia to new generations that would eventually succeed in overthrowing the Czar.

While Trone may have been inspired by the great political figure of Stepniak and the indefatigable Vera Figner, his life was nowhere near comparable to that of such heroes. While he was arrested twice for political activity, once in his school years and again in 1905, he was fairly detached from the world of radical politics.

Just before the 1917, approaching his fifties Trone had lived an interesting but in many respects a failed life. He was not a particularly successful engineer, political activist, husband, or even a corporate executive.

In school he did not excel in engineering studies. When he entered the workforce he failed utterly in his first job. Finding himself a known radical in Russia and therefore unable to find work, he went to Belgium. After some success in creating a ventilator protecting the health of workers at a dock in Antwerp, Trone was fired. He was fired for wasting his time in creating inventions when he should have been doing other things. No one had asked him to invent something to protect the workers' health; Trone just thought it was a good idea[6].

Trone then tried his hand working as an inventor. This was not a success either. Announcing proudly to his new boss that he had invented a marvellous machine Trone insisted on immediately switching it on. The boss took one look and realized, as marvellous as it was, it was probably quite dangerous and unstable. Once again Trone's ideals had raced ahead of the reality. His boss quickly ran for cover on the other side of the factory as Trone switched his machine on. Trone lost several teeth in the subsequent explosion.

His boss realized that Trone was at least as hardworking and knowledgeable an engineer as he was a failure when trying to put theory into practice. His Belgian employer realized that Trone should seek a different type of work, and went out immediately to find him alternative employment. The work his Belgian employer found was with General Electric. GE had just opened up operations in Russia. They needed a director who could oversee the work in Russia that GE in New York had been contracted to do.

Trone was somewhat hesitant to take the work. He knew he was not that good and he would be managing engineers with much greater skill and experience than himself. Trone may have had great ideals, but he certainly had a good deal of realism about his own skills to make those ideals possible. It was not long after taking the job that he told his engineers this. They in turn appreciated the honesty and that became the basis of a good working relationship. Many of the Bolsheviks who would come to power were one time employees of General Electric and its subsidiaries. Technically Trone as a Director, who would eventually be the president of the Russian General Electric, would be the one-time boss of those future leaders.

In the failed political uprising of 1905 Trone would see his lover and many of his comrades killed and he would end up in jail. With Trone's usual luck General Electric would just after the failed 1905 uprising promote Trone and bring him to their New York headquarters in Schenectady. He may not have been much of a success as their Russian agent or as a political activist, but he did have one thing that they really needed, intimate knowledge of Russia.

General Electric's headquarters in Schenectady proved to be a good place for a political radical like Trone to be. General Electric had moved its headquarters to Schenectady from New York City precisely to avoid radical socialist union influence upon its workers. Little did General Electric's executives know at the time that this would have the opposite effect than they desired. Many of their workers were the radical influence in trade unionism at the time. By taking the operation to a more isolated community, GE had created a perfectly friendly environment for Radicalism to flourish. Before long the workers in the town had elected a socialist mayor and started redesign the city based on socialist ideology. The union at General Electric would eventually become Communist in affiliation and ideology, all thanks to the isolated and friendly environment Schenectady provided[7].

For Trone after the 1905 Uprising, his transportation to Schenectady must have been like dying and going to heaven. In Schenectady he would make friends with one of the greatest engineers of the age, Charles Proteus Steinmentz. He would also enjoy the one thing he loved more than anything else; political discussions. Trone was fluently debating in English and winning those debates within two years of his arrival. He was also a short train ride to the meetings of political radicals in New York's Lower East Side.

For Trone life seemed idyllic but there was at least one tragedy. On one of the many journeys of Trone had taken while working in Russia his accompanying wife contracted Tuberculosis[8] and shortly died in the USA.

In some sense it could be said that by 1917 Trone was a failure. Only through luck had Trone survived so much of the disasters that plagued his life. It was the large scale and long term plans of General Electric and its powerful financial backers that had provided Trone a cushy life in Upstate New York. Here he could enjoy what he enjoyed the most. What he loved to do was talk. It was the one skill he had that seemed never to fail him and it was the single most important aspect in his life; his ability to be social and provide pleasant conversation.

Between 1917 and 1921 Trone's life of failure was propelled into the center of events that would change the world. There are traces of Trone appearing and disappearing in odd records around the world during this time period. What he did in that time is part legend and part spectacular truth.

To understand what happened in its entirety it's important to take a look at the events that occurred in the places he constantly traveled between in this time; to Lenin's political headquarters and Swope's General Electric.

Get With The Plan, Comrades!

At the Bolshoi Ballet Theatre, a location steeped in the history of high Russian culture, the leader of the new government stood up and delivered the last item on the agenda at that wintery meeting of the Communist party in December 1920. The last item on the agenda was a declaration that the time for politics was coming to an end and the real work was just beginning.

What was the real work of the new government? The real work would be industrial economic planning. The last item was a plan for the electrification of Russia on the American model, soon to be approved by GE engineers and financed by American capital. It was a plan that had been drafted by Trone's long-time friend, comrade and fellow electrical engineer Gleb Krzhizhanovsky[9].

It was purposely the last item on the agenda because it marked the end of the struggle to attain power and the moment they would begin exercising that power. All the old questions of how to win political power had been answered, and the dawn of a new age was upon them. This was not just a plan it was Lenin introducing a new era in Russian and even world history. A new way, a supposedly more enlightened way of doing things was being born. Lenin put the whole matter very simply:

> "Henceforth, less politics will be the best politics. Bring more engineers and agronomists to the fore, learn from them, keep an eye on their work, and turn our congresses and conferences, not into propaganda meetings but into bodies that will verify our economic achievements, bodies in which we can really learn the business of economic development[10]."

It was as if Lenin wished to turn his erstwhile political colleagues used to prisons, street fighting and writing propaganda into businessmen; executive directors who would approve the plans created and executed by their industrial managers. Lenin's ideal moved Russia from a medieval power structure dependent upon an autocracy guided directly, so it was widely believed, by the will of God to one that looked more like bureaucratic boardrooms full of powerful executives on Wall Street in New York City. Of course these directors would be working primarily to bring, in theory, benefits to the people and the new government, the ultimate shareholders in these corporations.

Perhaps more startling than this transition of political activists to Businessmen was the transition proposed for the vast bulk of the people of Russia. No longer would they be illiterate superstitious peasants languishing in the oblivion of ignorance, they would become modern corporate employees. They would be highly literate and cultivated, enjoy all the facilities and benefits of the rich in the big cities.

Interesting to note is that many of the Bolshevik leadership at this time went as far as to say that they needed "An American-Russian" someone who would have one foot in both worlds to help the rest of the former Russian Empire make the transition[11]. Such a person Trone could be considered. The transition of course would require more than just a few American Russians.

Russia at the time was a mess not just because of the millions dead or injured by the First World War. In Russia almost a third of children died before they got to five. If one did survive childhood, one could not possibly expect to make it to thirty-five, unless one lived as a rich landlord. During what small life one had almost everyone would be illiterate having less education than one might get in a primary school. The few who did know how to read and write were mostly living in Moscow or Petrograd; far away from the peasant farm in the middle of nowhere. Roads, housing, sanitation, hospitals, schools, libraries, factories, electric power, tractors, or just about anything that was making life better in the rest of Europe were as otherworldly to Russians as the Kingdom of Heaven, where most of them hoped to go after a short miserable life.

Russia at the beginning of the 20th century was a wretched and miserable corner of Europe filled with disease, ignorance and oppression. On top of this, ensuring nothing would change was a government structure dedicated to ideals that had not changed in a thousand years. To say mismanaged is to put the matter lightly. The Czar had autocratic control of every aspect of the government. By European standards the population was heavily taxed, very poor and subject to frequent famines. What industries that did exist in Russia were overwhelmingly owned either by the Czar or foreign business interests. Ethnic minorities fared even worse. Russian imperial policy enforced numerous repressive laws to harass ethnic minorities, often forcing them to adopt Russian culture and language just to survive.

In a few years Lenin hoped his fellow citizens would be just as developed if not more so than those who lived in the United States. With the electrification of his country, just like turning on a light bulb, Russia would find itself transported into an enlightened world. The example of the United States, gave Lenin and his Bolsheviks hope that such a transformation was possible.

The Americans had started to leave their farms at the end of the last century and in a short time were now mostly punching time clocks and working on assembly lines under the strict instructions and supervision of their managers experts, engineers in the new technology. It was as if Lenin had made the plea to all the peoples of the former Russian Empire, to rebuild their country in the image of the United States.

Lenin showed himself to be a true disciple of American efficiency and technology demonstrating how a plan would make their society function in harmony:

> "Without a plan of electrification, we cannot undertake any real constructive work. When we discuss the restoration of agriculture, industry and transport, and their harmonious coordination, we are obliged to discuss a broad economic plan. We must adopt a definite plan...Only when the country has been electrified, and industry, agriculture and transport have been placed on the technical basis of modern large-scale industry, only then shall we be fully victorious...The plan must be carried out at all costs, and its deadline brought nearer.[12]"

A plan for electrification had been requested early in 1920. Technical experts, Russia's best that had not fled the country, were brought together to create a plan for electrification. Trone of course was there from the start. How much he contributed we do not know. However some years later while chatting casually with the U.S. ambassador to Latvia in an unannounced visit he did reveal some interesting if not unexpected statements. The ambassador reported that, "He stated that when Russians first began to industrialize the country, they purchased ready made plans and designs for the construction of plants from American companies[13]."

Why did the Soviets pick American designs for their industrialization? The answer from Trone was equally unexpected as it was unflattering to the American ambassador, "The Russians believe that conditions in their country roughly approximate those in the United States during its period of industrial development, in that they have a large potential market, great natural resources and an inexhaustible supply of unskilled labour[14]."

America was at one time full of illiterate peasants living in a comparatively untouched wilderness similar to how Russia was in 1917. The land and the people contained a great potential for development. The territories of the former Russian Empire could be developed to unleash its great potential to supply the basis for the most highly civilized people the world had known. If America could develop itself so far out of nothing so would Russia.

It is not because that the United States was so advanced, which it was, that the Bolsheviks borrowed their plans from the United States, on the contrary, it is because the Americans had been so backward in so many ways. The plans for Russia's development were taken from a land founded and developed by a great mass of illiterate peasants.

The United States was on the whole a success story. It had liberated itself from European control, and its population was now educated and largely composed of affluent industrial professionals using high technology to develop themselves and their society further. What started off as poor European immigrants with little or no education farming in a wilderness had become one of the most powerful countries in the world with a highly sophisticated population. Lenin intended for Russia to be re-founded as the Soviet Union in the same way. If the United States could develop itself with peasants why could not Russia do the same if not better?

Gleb Krzhizhanovsky, the Bolshevik, considered to be the father of Soviet Planning, had independently looked at the development of industrial societies such as Germany, Britain and the United States. He knew that the American offered the best equivalent, on the surface, because it was so close in size and qualities to that of the former Russian Empire. It is no surprise therefore that by the end of 1920 the Bolsheviks under Lenin were moving forward in the direction promoted by Swope and Trone.

There was a definite reason why they had thought Russia could be transformed into a new version of America. The reason was firsthand knowledge.

Many of them had become exiles in the United States and had seen the development first hand. They had seen rough Russian peasant immigrants arriving in New York City, becoming in the space of months industrial workers, adapting themselves with few difficulties to a new reality.

Russian political exiles in general had been visiting the United States for almost a century. A long and rich history of American adventures had developed. In the 1840s the Russian Anarchist Bakunin had escaped from his imprisonment in Siberia, crossed the Pacific and traveled across the West from San Francisco to find a warm reception in Boston. In Boston Bakunin had stated that the Russia he wanted to build would be like the United States. The father of modern Anarchism saw the United States as his ideal. Later exiles would gain a similar appreciation of the United

States. To Russians of the Nineteenth Century the United States was the land of political sympathy and an example to be emulated[15].

The Bolshevik acceptance of Swope's American planning ideals is not a mystery. The Russian exiles love of America was a tradition deeply engrained in Lenin's Bolsheviks. These enemies of Capital were in love with the long term broad industrial planning process and the benefits it promised to give the former territories of the Czar. Large corporate planning was the ultimate goal of the Bolshevik state. Trone whose career was dedicated to creating long term plans found in the Bolsheviks great partners who would give him the scope to take it to the highest level possible. As Trone said about his work for Lenin, "You spoiled me in Russia[16]." The Soviet Union may not have been the Workers' Paradise, but it certainly was in those early days a planner's paradise.

Betting Against the Future

An important question remains. Why did capitalists find colluding with the Bolsheviks increasingly attractive? As we have seen the Bolsheviks represented a new way to get money out of a bad loan. The acceptance of planning by the Bolsheviks however was meant to put an end to foreign dependence, to make the former Russian Empire stand on its own without dependence on capitalists. Surely this was not the basis of a long term relationship?

The Bolsheviks wanted to be "fully victorious" which in their ideology meant freedom from capitalists. The Bolsheviks were creating corporate directors just like in the U.S., but these were "Red Directors." These Red Directors had their ultimate goal in increasing the political power of the Bolsheviks, not primarily the capital of the external investors.

The Bolshevik theorist Nikolai Bukharin put the matter perhaps a little too simply when he said, "Thus capitalism, driving the concentration of production to extraordinary heights, and having created a centralized production apparatus, has therewith prepared the immense rank: of its own grave-diggers. In the great clash of classes, the dictatorship of finance capital is being replaced by the dictatorship of the revolutionary proletariat."

Now the Bolsheviks were borrowing from the American capitalist corporations both intellectually and financially, but how long would it be before these corporate minded business-like political radicals removed their rivals? Profitable as this relationship promised to be, the alliance was temporary and highly tenuous. How long would it be until they reverted to the actions of the Russian activists of old who did not care for making business deals and preferred acts of individual retribution against capitalists?

Of course capitalists are used to working with their competitors. Upon occasion capitalists will even work in a temporary alliance with those whose ultimate aim is to push them out of the market and bankrupt them if necessary. Temporary alliances like this for short term benefits between competitors are not uncommon.

American business interests had employed those with openly strong political sympathies such as Trone, Steinmetz and Swope. However employing these radicals to create a new and powerful state for the Bolshevik leadership, may have seemed a step too far. It was risky and only a person who liked extreme risks would take it. Such a man was Gerard Swope.

In Swope's authorized biography that he edited shortly before his death, he made it clear that he knew from the start there would be many objections to his taking over General Electric. Swope knew he was too rough a personality and too radical and dangerous in his ideas[17].

To answer the first objection was a simple matter of buying him a public face or front to mask the unsavoury character of the real manager of General Electric. That mask was a second person who would do all the socializing. That person was the lawyer Owen D. Young who was well known for his gentle and disarmingly folksy manners. Both Swope and Young would share a co-presidency, but while Young would do the talking, Swope would do all the working. Swope characteristically spelled this out very bluntly for Young when he started. Young found no objection to the arrangement[18].

To the second challenge, that he was too radical, Swope had a double response. His methods were immediately profitable and secondly this was the way things had to be done in the future. The old way of paying cash up front for merchandise was over. Now the business would deal in long term business arrangements, cultivating industries and planning on a large even global scale of development.

The first most virulent attack on Swope's new methods was, not surprisingly, his deal with the new government of Russia. The business community did not like it, and were afraid of its consequences. Swope was well aware of this anger.

> There was angry comment that the Russians couldn't be trusted to pay, and also that help in industrialization was raising up a dangerous enemy to the Capitalist system[19].

Swope was a born gambler. He loved to gamble and he especially loved to gamble with other people's money. When he offered his clients credits to be paid back over the long term, he was betting on the power of his machines. He knew the machines he was selling, such as electrical turbine power generators, would generate power to run industries, which would buy more of his machines, to run factories and farms and generate profit over the long term. He was in the business of speculating that his clients would be able to achieve great success over the long term, because that is precisely what his machines were designed to do[20].

If you could afford the power generators straight away you probably did not need them. GE's power generating machines were designed for regions that did not have power to support an industry that could afford to buy his machines.

Swope knew his superior product would always have the upper hand over his impoverished clients. They would be generating profit only in the long term; they would be indebted to Swope because of this. By the time they had paid off the machines, the technology would have advanced significantly so that to keep competitive they would have to buy more and newer machines. His clients were not just buying machines they were becoming forever in Swope's debt. The only chance they would have is to industrialize quicker than Swope anticipated and to pay for the next generation of technology without getting into debt. This was the gamble, a gamble Swope thought he would win.

Swope loved to speculate on the future, and he liked the stakes to be high. His authorized biography makes this quite clear:

> He preferred not to call his successful ventures speculation and his own have been generally successful that he feels he really has not been a speculator at all. With such talk a man of strong gambling tastes can conceal himself from himself[21].

Swope in 1953, in a taped transcript, shortly before he died, said he knew Russia and knew what state she was in when they had developed their plans. He said he was personally involved and to a much greater extent than he would normally in the first agreements with the new Russia under the Bolsheviks. The development of the electrification process was dependent upon the ability to procure Electrical Generators such as those produced by GE. The Bolsheviks wanted to rebuild Russia's industry on American lines.

When Swope went to Russia, he must have seen perfectly that he had a land ripe for his technology, and a buyer for that technology that intended to make the most of it. Now Russia would be built with American industries such as International Harvester, RCA and most important of all General Electric[22].

That the trade would grow to hundreds of thousands of dollars, tens of billions in today's money was an estimate that came to pass. The trade did grow by at a rate that far over shadowed the debt that was forgiven. By 1930 the purchase for that year alone of US products was over $114 million[23], around $23 billion if applying an economy cost estimation of today's values. The debt for these purchases made the USSR dependent on the technology they had purchased for their future development.

The two people who made this dream come true for American business were primarily Swope and Trone. As we have seen Swope was the originator of the plan, but it was Trone who would be the man responsible for making that plan come to life in Russia.

To know exactly what Trone was doing at this time we have to see what was said in a State Department report in the 1950s. In a confidential report of an FBI interview dated April 25th 1951 a GE executive who appears to be Clark Haynes Minor said:

> He said he could not conceive of Trone's being involved in espionage activity. That the subject in the past furnished technical information to the Russians he did not doubt, for the reason that Trone was sent to Russia for that express purpose, namely to aid in the development of Russian industry during the various five year plans. This according to the unnamed informant was done with the approval of the United States Government[24].

This information was repeated almost exactly as to Trone's activities by the President of General Electric after Swope retired Charles Wilson when interviewed by the FBI.

> Trone knew every leading person and he made it a business for himself to be interested in all research so he had hoped to build up the Soviet Industries with General Electric patterns which were carried to the Soviet Union.[25]

Corporate executives and financial interests had no doubt trusted in the deal partly because it was the best way to recoup losses but also because Swope, although a political radical, had shown the way to future profits. In an interview in the 1930s Clark Haynes Minor had stated that

> We disregarded the two-million dollar Czarist debts and never regretted having forgotten them. Indirectly we recovered the claim amply. We went on the theory that if a person wants credit he must take certain risks, especially if a great area like Russia had to be industrialized[26].

Gerard Swope knew Russia and he took an assessment of her capabilities before he signed the deal:

> My thought was that it would take at least a generation to transform an agricultural people into an industrial one, and if we kept our leadership in engineering and manufacturing, at the end of that period we would still be in the lead[27].

He opposed the concept, which in his industry was notably a German one, that other countries would be prevented from developing their own heavy industry. He preferred, he said, to take the risk of competition, confident that continued progress in research and education would preserve American technical and productive leadership better than attempts to maintain a technical or productive monopoly.

Swope's whole plan was dependent upon two factors, one was the money it would immediately bring in and the other was the secondary manufacturing role it would give Russia. Swope bet that Russia would get America's manufacturing technology and become a manufacturing economy while the United States and the West would become the masters of high technology.

The West would keep the brains, the capital and the controls and Lenin's Russia would be a subservient, feeder economy, giving us their manufactured products. Russia would always, so Swope hoped, remain entirely dependent upon the West for the manufacturing technology itself that ran their factories. They did all the hard work and the West would remain a powerful partner getting all the profits. Lenin was not unaware of the nature of this bet. It was a bet Swope almost lost and Lenin almost won.

It is interesting to note that later in life when Trone was sending a letter seeking employment as industrial advisor to Prime Minister Nehru of India he had a chance to say what he had learned throughout his long career in planning:

> I am aware of the need for industrial planning as the basis for economic and social progress ... I have learnt, too, that foreign experience cannot be copied mechanically, but must be understood, digested and adapted to local realities, and that short-range and long-range planning must be interconnected[28].

To Trone there was a problem with planning generally and that problem went back to his initial experience working with the Russians. The methods for one would not work for another. Copying and borrowing from the powerful meant being in the debt of the powerful. Trone would try and sadly fail to come up with an entirely successful alternative. As we shall see however, Trone was far from seeing himself as defeated and would continue with some incredible successes to tilt the bet in favor of his political sympathies.

Endnotes

1   (Ilf and Petrov 1937, 41)
2   (Roth January 27, 1951); (Trone, et al. 2009)
3   (Trone, et al. 2009)
4   (Trone, et al. 2009)
5   (Schmidt 2008)
6   (Trone, et al. 2009)
7   (Zahavi September, 1996)
8   (Trone, et al. 2009)
9   (Trone, et al. 2009)
10   (V. Lenin December 22, 1920)
11   (Rogger July 1981); (K. E. Bailes July 1981); (Dorn 1979)
12   (V. Lenin December 22, 1920)
13   (S. Trone, State Department Solomon Trone Interview 1933)
14   (S. Trone, State Department Solomon Trone Interview 1933)
15.   (Handlin 1942)
16   (Ilf and Petrov 1937, 41)
17   (Loth 1958, 1-3)
18   (Loth 1958, 3)
19   (Loth 1958, 185)
20   (Loth 1958, 185)
21   (Loth 1958, 49)
22   (Hoff 1974, 83)
23   (Hoff 1974, 83)
24   (Federal Bureau of Investigations 1951)
25   (Hoover, FBI Correspondence to Nicholson 1951)
26   (Hoff 1974, 94)
27   (Loth 1958, 185)
28   (S. Trone, Brief Outline of my Engineering Experience 1949)

Chapter 4

THE END OF REASON

The View from Desolation Row

"**N**o, no, gentlemen!" said Solomon Trone, "It will not take very long." He sat himself squarely on the dark oak chair as if he were a king ascending to his throne[1].

At his insistence the prison guards did all the regular procedures as they would with any condemned prisoner, leaving nothing out. The straps were attached to his torso, head, legs and arms. Wide thick leather belts were used.

There was a silence when all the straps were attached. No one wanted to carry out the final procedure; placing the electric connection cap to Solomon Trone's freshly shaved head. Once again Trone insisted, and the guards quietly went about their usual business and attached the electric cap to his head. No one moved, not his wife, not the prison guards, no one. Solomon Trone smiled a full broad smile and showed every sign of satisfaction. It was as if this was something that he had to do.

A witness to the event said, "It was evident at once that he was one of those people who want to do everything, who want to touch everything with their hands, to see and hear everything themselves[2]."

Trone was visiting Sing-Sing Prison in New York, and asked to see its infamous death chamber. It was there that United States federal government executed its prisoners by method of electric chair; one of Edison's most notorious of inventions. When Trone got there and the guards showed him the chair, he had asked to be able to sit in the chair. No one had asked this before, but the guards were happy to oblige the visitor.

What the guards and his fellow visitors did not know was how close Solomon Trone had come, and would come, to some of the most publicized executions in the preceding decade. Friends, colleagues and comrades had gone in an endless line to trials that were little more than theatrical performances leading to the main event; the public execution. He had seen the innocent murdered and some of them had been murdered here, where he sat, lashed with leather belts to a chair. He saw what they had seen, the men he had been unable to save, that his electricity, the force of enlightenment, had scorched and blasted with lethal jolts. Whether they had been murdered by those professing the ideology of Fascism, Capitalism or Communism, they had all died without guilt, without the truth being known, for reasons no one at the time could quite understand.

As public as the trials and executions had been, the reasons remained obscure and twisted in ever deepening plots and intrigues. No one knew why or how they ended up, facing death and condemnation, they were just there, and they were the right shape, size and quality needed to fill a grave.

To Trone, death was not the important factor and never would be. It was the lies. If you go down the road of executions to meet your goals, willingly or not, do not force the truth so far underground that it lies buried deeper than the corpse of the executed. Trone if anything valued knowledge, the search for the truth. This was his job; to talk to everyone he could, know scientifically the world around him and then come to some approximation of the way things were and how they could be improved. This was the essence of planning, a clear and free appraisal of the way things are and what they could be.

For Trone if you execute the truth, you executed the future; it took away his ability to plan for the development of a better world. The truth had become a casualty in the war of ideologies that erupted in the twenties and thirties. Today's heroes would become tomorrow's traitors. Specifically it was the planners and the plans that were both being executed, and these executions were very close to heart of Trone.

The very plans that Trone had worked on had become the subject of ideological warfare. The plans to industrialize the former territories of the Czar were seen as both great crimes and tremendous achievements. Since Trone had initially worked with the Bolsheviks until he left the Soviet Union in 1932, the planning process had turned the country on its head. The development of industry had sky rocketed and looked as though its progress would continue eventually outstripping the West in industrial power.

The cost had had also been massive. The Soviets were now a power to be feared, this was not the old Czarist Russia, but the beginnings of powerful industrial state. Its once illiterate masses were now ninety percent literate. The massive death rate common to Russia was cut in half, diseases had been wiped out, and transportation bridged the massive isolating distances. In every field of human endeavor it appeared the Soviets were out pacing everyone, moving from a medieval society to a vast industrial state of unstoppable development.

The execution of Solomon Trone's plans however was soon met with the execution of Solomon Trone's fellow planners. In the West the threat of the Soviet Union brought forth its own executions and established states that were little more than military encampments with only one rabid over riding desire, the destruction of Bolshevism even if it meant their own destruction.

By the mid-1930s it was clear to Solomon Trone when the next World War would begin. Long before that point, and long before he saw his friends led into the oblivion of concentration camps and execution, Solomon Trone understood that there was a danger arising that had to be confronted.

As always Trone did not accept second hand accounts; he would go into the heart of the danger and see for himself. As we will see the only protection he took with him was his ability to talk. So amazing was this ability that even his most determined assassin would falter in the act and be unable to stop him. Solomon Trone would survive bearing witness to the truth he had seen, although it was a truth almost no one was willing to listen to.

When Trone sat in the Electric Chair he was seeing past the executions to see what was to come, something more deadly, of a greater magnitude of disaster. As sinister as the trials and executions had been Trone knew they were merely the first step, he knew precisely where it would lead.

Trone was a planner; he envisioned a world in the future from what existed today. The executions, imprisonments and exiles of the last decade were targeted to eliminate the most intelligent and independent voices in such societies as Germany, the U.S. and Russia. With these people gone, without the intelligent critical spirit they provided, these nations were marching unhindered by either reason or compassion toward a senseless global confrontation. Trone knew this because he and his fellow engineers had effectively given the power of advanced technology to leaders far too incompetent to control it and far too malevolent to create any good from it.

With these executions Trone saw clearly where it would lead. Without the ability to use the new technology wisely and with compassion, these societies were operating blind; it could only lead to disaster. With the accuracy of seer Trone predicted that a global conflict would break out in 1939. These executions would lead directly to that conflict, try as he might to prevent it or stem some of the damage, Trone recognized that without the critical control necessary the new technological power and its development would be the only element that would dictate what and when future events would occur.

The Sickle Pays for the Hammer

In the early days of Lenin's government it was clear the debt for industrialization plans had the ability to cripple the society. A society remains poor unless it can industrialize; to industrialize you need to take on massive debts. There was little option but to industrialize as fast as possible, so that the debt could be paid off before it ruined the state. It was a race against time.

The initial payments came from two things Russia had immediately at hand to sell to the West. One was items of cultural heritage, such as religious icons and the other was grain.

Lenin had allowed in the American relief agencies in the early twenties to help feed the famine victims of the Soviet Union. Production and farming had almost been driven to a halt by the First World War, the Revolution, the Foreign Intervention armies and the Civil War. Now after all that was over, or at least coming to an end, there was famine across the land and the country needed help get back on its feet. This is something that Trone and the other planners made quite clear as the main problem facing Russia.

To get that help the American government stepped forward, as they had done so generously before, and donated as well as donating massive amounts of grain and other food supplies to halt the starvation they considered also helping the new state of the Soviet Union develop its industrial capacity. Lenin knew a good thing when he saw it. The offer he put forward through his government was that the "Soviet government is exceptionally interested in any step which could bring closer economic relations between Russia and the United States. It goes without saying that these economic relations should rest [on the basis of equality and mutual interest[3]."

What had transpired though was a mix of strategies from the US government. Some sections had wanted to help rebuild Russia and thereby forge a closer alliance while others wanted the opposite. In practical terms this disjointed and contradictory set of policies was in effect. Material assistance was being given to people in the Soviet Union as well as to the White Army that was at that time trying to overthrow it[4].

While the Soviet Union benefited from this divided approach by the United States, it was clear the situation would not last nor be repeated if there was another famine.

In the days of the Czar a grain shortage worldwide meant often profits for some agricultural interest within Russia. Instead of seeking the means to prevent further famine there was a very limited and conflicted understanding by the Russian Intelligentsia under the old Czarist Empire as to how to combat famine when it occurred as well as taking steps in preventing its occurrence. As the country was subject to massive deaths through famine the economy saw very slight changes to its trade and savings[5]. Russia before Lenin was not facing the difficulties that had to be surmounted.

Lenin as well as Trone and his fellow industrial planners were more than aware that previous lack of investment in modernizing technology had been a major cause of the famines. This time they would buy machines, machines to produce more grain, steel, factories and above all power. To do this they would use what they had on hand which was amongst other things grain.

When famine did occur again in the Soviet Union from 1932-1933 grain exports were still being exported despite desperate need for the grain in the Soviet Union[6]. This famine disproportionately affected the grain growing region of Ukraine. The situation was not remedied until it was too late to prevent its occurrence.

The leader at the time Josef Stalin was opposed to increasing grain exports in September 1931. Also the Soviets were secretly clandestinely buying grain off the foreign markets to combat the famine as it was occurring[7].

The Soviet Union had to pay its debts and seem viable in the long run so it could keep borrowing off the market, for this reason it had to buy the amounts of grain it was losing in secret.

The grain was of course needed in the Soviet Union, rather than being converted to hard currency to pay General Electric and other foreign investors. Swope however said with glowing pride, that the Soviets under Stalin paid the debt "punctually and punctiliously"[8]. This payment on the debt and on new orders could have been used to build food reserves for the famine. Instead such as it 1929 it contributed to one of the most profitable years General Electric had ever known outside of war time[9].

Of course in a number of ways it was a war that provided these profits; a geopolitical war, a class war, a war between the starving peasants and the Soviet state, a war between the debtor and the holder of the debt; this was a "total war" in the sense that it involved an entire society. As the rest of the world plunged into a severe economic depression in 1929 GE was doing just fine.

The industrialization of Russia was a virtual take off. It's an unprecedented event in the history of mankind. It was remarkable in itself that it had gone from a very low position economically and technically. They had caught up and modernized. They were an advanced industrial economy by the 1930s competing with other advanced industrial economies. Largely their economic position was on par if not ahead of their closest military and economic rivals, such as Germany[10].

By the 1930s the effects of the initial planning by Trone and the experts and the hard work and sacrifices of the Soviet people finally saw its payoff in such things as houses, roads, transportation, medicine, and cultural facilities. The important aspects of providing a good life for the people became better. There was a real sense of purpose and satisfaction in the achievements felt throughout society.

There was also an underlying nervousness by the government of the power the planners and technical experts had been given to make this possible[11]. Often directly part of foreign operations such as those run by General Electric they would become obvious targets of a government determined to reduce the power of this group as a privileged and powerful class.

As the government moved to consolidate its control it started to remove the independent planners, directors and experts from their positions of power. Some of these were the very oldest and closest associates and friends of Trone. As these trials progressed Trone would be given a seat in the courtroom that condemned such experts.

The Show Must Go On

Andrey Vyshinsky was an engineer and a friend of Trone from his days before the fall of the Czar. They corresponded with each other throughout their lives until Vyshinsky's death in the 1950s in New York City as a Trade Ambassador from the Soviet Union[12]. He was a former Menshevik, the opposing faction in the Russian Social-Democratic Labour Party, to Lenin's Bolsheviks. During the months between the fall of the Czar and the October Revolution of the Bolsheviks he held an important position within the Provisional Government. At one point in the Provisional government he signed the warrant for the arrest of Lenin. At the storming of the Winter Palace, he was one of the Winter Palace defenders against the Bolsheviks.

As Trone's friend, and one time political ally, it is of some surprise to find that he would be the judge. The fortunes of time had come around so that now Vyshinsky would be the judge and hold a verdict of so many of the Bolsheviks who had triumphed over him. He has been credited with being the legal mastermind behind the Stalin purges. Despite being the judge who presided so willingly over Stalin's court, damning scores to exile, prison and execution, never did he face judgment himself.

The prosecutor would have a different fate, one that, as some have commented, was poetic. The prosecutor Nikolai Krylenko would later, under the same type of torture with which he interrogated others, confess to being an enemy of Lenin since 1917. He would also claim his involvement in sabotaging Soviet industry. There was a few years to go however before this confession would come out, leading to his execution after a twenty minute trial.

The most important trial he would prosecute would be anything but quick and silent; it would be big and broadcast to the nation. This trial was against a group called "The Industrial Party"[13]. The trial would be the first one broadcast live throughout the Soviet Union.

This would be a "show-trial." It was a show trial because it took place with all the public as witnesses. It was also an entirely staged performance. As with so much in Russian history, the great works of fiction often resemble factual reality, and that which is supposed to be factual, such as trial for treason, was nothing more than fiction on a grand scale. Krylenko would be one of the main actors in that fiction.

The main star of the performance was the chief defendant; a man whose denunciation of himself, his extravagant claims of wickedness, have rarely ever been matched in fiction. He painted his supposed villainies so vast and iniquitous that it appalled the imagination, and made sure that the listening Soviet public was entertained by a tale of profound and creative wickedness. Without any doubt if one man could be said to have reveled in the badness of the event it was this man. His name was Leonid Ramzin; a well-known heating scientist and engineer, the creator of the direct-flow steam boiler. He was one of the early protégé of Solomon Trone. He had followed Trone back to the Soviet workshop provided by General Electric in Schenectady. He was one of the brightest and most gifted of the engineers that the Bolsheviks had used to plan and design the Soviet Union's mammoth industrial development.

Dr. Leonid Konstantinovich Ramzin was born in 1887 in the village of Sosnovka in Tambov province. His parents were school teachers. In 1898 he graduated from Tambov Boys grammar school. He was trained in mathematics by Aleksandrova the famed political radical and pioneer in mathematics. He greatly contributed to the plans for the electrification of the Soviet Union. In this work he traveled for studying and operational experience to England, Belgium, Germany, Czechoslovakia, the most extensively to the USA. He was also largely associated with the refitting of the Moscow power generating stations to use local fuel. In 1927 he moved to work on the development of the first Five Year Plan.

During the trial Ramzin was the self-declared head of the Industrial party criminal gang that of course did not exist. No one else spoke for the defendants. The rest just sat there and listened to the story of Ramzin the leader and his Industrial Party. There crimes were supposedly spectacular and defied not only conventional logic but also the laws of time and space as well. The crimes also ranged from the fantastic to the mind-numbingly mundane.

The first and foremost of their crimes, that everything else was built on, was that they had followed last year's budget and plan to the letter; filling their quotas and making sure that Bolshevik leaders had their orders executed to the letter. They had done their job well, which apparently was a terrible crime for which no torture or imprisonment would be enough to rectify. Of course if they had not followed orders they too would have committed a crime only their deaths could rectify.

Ramzin said they were actively working in an organization to disrupt Soviet development. They were wrecking production by supporting production that took resources away from the main Soviet planning goals. What this meant was that as they were following the plans that they were ordered to follow. Consequently they were not following the orders and plans for the next year, which had not been given yet, which would have been absurd. Those future plans may contradict the previous plans. Like a normal planning process, the previous plans are always taken into account. What worked, what didn't? Some things worked well and others proved unprofitable. So plans change, and in the normal course of events orders change from year to year. However in this situation, using Stalin's logic, as the plans changed it meant everything this supposed criminal gang under Ramzin did in the previous year was in effect sabotage and therefore high treason.

But sabotage for what purpose? They were apparently sabotaging production by draining the swamps in the Southern Ukraine, as they had been ordered to do by the Bolsheviks, in order so the French government could land its troops and invade Russia. This of course was absurd and after the trial Stalin's government was forced by the French government, under threat of trade sanctions, to withdraw the assertion.

This fictional but fiendish plan was to drain entire agricultural regions of unproductive swamps. In doing so it was really done to allow a non-existent French invasion force to enter the Soviet Union. This plan was apparently hatched in Paris with an Official Agent of the Czar and the French Prime Minister. The Czarist Official who Ramzin said he spoke with in Paris had been dead for a number of years. So these people in the criminal gang had followed the official orders of Stalin in order so a massive French army led by a living dead Czarist Official could invade. To this charge all the defendants said they were guilty. The defendants other than Ramzin were not allowed to say anything else other than guilty.

On the whole, as a broadcast theatrical performance, the production itself would be more highly rated than the previous Shakhty trial, which had been somewhat of a warm up. The trial was better staged than the Shakhty trial from 1928 which had more dead people doing things and also a good number of logical impossibilities. The other advantage over the Shakhty trial was its live broadcast throughout the Soviet Union. As other trials would occur, this one would still be remembered the most deeply by the Russian people. This is the original model for the show-trial and as such it still holds a deep cultural memory for the Russian people.

The opinion both then and now, from the political left and right, including Trotsky after originally being fooled by it, is that Stalin wanted his men in the key planning positions. The condemned men were all in those key planning positions and they were not political agents of Stalin, many of them were not political at all, they merely wished to do the work in which they were experts. Of course Stalin's people were politically loyal and not planning experts. Trone of course knew all of the accused. Trone would get even to see the trial from the foreign visitors' seats in the courtroom[14].

Solomon Trone's son, Dmitri Trone who had been assigned by his father as the official head of General Electric in Russia sent his father a press cutting from the New York Times. Dmitri numbered each one of the people in the picture that appeared in the New York Times regarding the Industrial Party Trial. Like a good engineer Dmitri meticulously numbers and names each person he knew in the picture, including his father, who is in the center and of course listed as number one.

All the defendants except for Ramzin were executed either immediately or in the massive purge of '37. Ramzin went into a "prison" more like an upscale hotel replete with his own laboratory and was rehabilitated in 1932. He later got several top honours including the Stalin Award, the Lenin Award and the Order of the Red Banner. Ramzin later joked with others about the trial saying it was all straight from Stalin. Ramzin knew he would get the soft treatment and eventually get to rise to the top of his profession, if he played his part well. Obviously Stalin did feel he had played his part well. Ramzin eventually died of natural causes in 1948.

As other trials were to follow the pattern had been set. The independent thinkers, the men who were loyal to the truth and their moral principals were selected and executed. This created a spiral of incompetence from the top to the bottom of Soviet society. Most critically of all the blind subservience to authority led to a lag of technical development between the Soviets and the West. Even after the death of Stalin, this was something the Soviets were not able to fully overcome. Areas such as genetics and computer technology, where the Soviet's would initially lead would be discarded as pseudo-science. The West would develop these technologies improving their industries and economies.

This technical lag would ensure that the development of the Soviet Union would fulfill Gerard Swope's prophesy. Manufacturing technology requiring the hard labour of industrial workers would be shifted to Soviet style secondary economies such as we see now in China, where people would have a lower standard of living. The power of course, with the technological edge would remain with the West. Swope's global economy of two tier development was practically ensured by Stalin's efforts to consolidate his power and eliminate Trone's independent planners.

While Trone was impressed by the industrial development of the Soviet Union, he was not surprisingly soon butting heads with the Soviet elites. The Soviet historian Tarle came in for specific rebuke from Trone. "You old whore Tarle," shouted Trone at a party, "why don't you write about the revolution the way it really happened?" Tarle shrugged and answered, "It's alright for you; you don't live here.[15]"

When in New York a few years later he wrote a letter into *The Nation* magazine. He said that the Soviet Union was a land being built by young motivated people[16]. He did not mention the purges in the article; unlike in the Soviet Union, where he risked everything by condemning the purges continually[17]. He was not blind to what was happening, he was however becoming more isolated both in the USA and the USSR partly because of the purges.

At this point Solomon Trone decided that the answer to the world's problems must exist, if it did anywhere, outside of Europe and America. To this end he planned yet another trip around the world. This time he would take his new wife who he had just married. She, Florence had fluency in a number of languages and her prior career as his secretary, meant she would be able to help Solomon in his investigations. The Trones would travel the world looking for someone reasonable to talk to. As he would tell Swope in a letter a few years later,

> I have spent a good deal of time during the last few years travelling slowly on freighters to different parts of the world, thus satisfying my old urge to understand the causes of unrest and of the awful changes that are taking place. I have, among other places, spent long periods of time in France, Italy, (and) Palestine. I have, as I think, learnt a great deal and am still learning[18].

Fear in a Handful of Dust

In London in 1922 a Harvard educated American banker looked over the newspapers and read about the Versailles Treaty. He read about the enormous financial debt that the allies had forced on the defeated Germany. The American banker had a responsibility in his work to collect business intelligence, as much as he could. With his multitude of languages and his extraordinary even legendary intuition he would get to the bottom of world events, and connect up all the dots. Everything would eventually make sense under his scrutiny and then he would deliver his daily report to the corporation.

This particular morning however, he was not feeling very clever. He was not feeling much except a terrible numbness of all sensation. The news had hit him hard. His work that day was rendered meaningless by the news he had just read. There was little business intelligence to gather, it was all too obvious, too crude and grotesque. He could see clearly where the massive debt would lead. His beloved England, the romantic island he loved as only a rich foreigner can was destined with the rest of Western Europe to a fate he would rather not contemplate.

This was a morning where he would not be seeking the truth, but trying to evade it. As much as he tried, the Harvard educated banker could not. He would eventually put aside his financial books and set about writing a poem as the only way to properly express the situation, in all its complexity and sadness.

What was eventually produced was not a happy poem. "I will show you fear in a handful of dust." This was not your usual business language. He was quite clear that something had been lost and some unspeakable horror had been born, "...I could not Speak, and my eyes failed, I was neither Living nor dead, and I knew nothing." He saw those around him as walking casualties, or as ones condemned; nothing could save them. Something had happened that made every word come too short to explain the horror of it.

> A crowd flowed over London Bridge, so many,
> I had not thought death had undone so many.
> Sighs, short and infrequent, were exhaled,
> And each man fixed his eyes before his feet.

The crisis was upon them, the guns of the First World War and Revolution had stopped but the crisis was only gathering strength in the pause; nothing had been achieved, the long decline was leading to an end that was all too clear. "The nymphs are departed. And their friends, the loitering heirs of city directors; Departed, have left no addresses." The War and the Revolution had cracked the essence of his gentle, comfortable and romantic existence at the heart of a once rich empire. The anglophile Harvard banker knew that the dream was over, and this empire of wealth in Western Europe was coming to an end. Germans, French and British were all in a very real sense equally defeated.

These imperial powers were wrecked to a point from which they could not recover. The banker had done the math and knew that the numbers for the first time in three hundred years were not in the favor of Western European countries. These were all effectively bankrupt societies whether they realized it or not, no matter how they juggled the debt or tried to limit the damage to one country, that being Germany. In truth he felt they had refused to see what he could see only too clearly when he looked over the Versailles Treaty.

> Prison and palace and reverberation
> Of thunder of spring over distant mountains
> He who was living is now dead
> We who were living are now dying

With a little patience

Using the word "city," which has a double meaning in London and usually refers to its financial industry, the banker says, "What is the city over the mountains / Cracks and reforms and bursts in the violet air / Falling towers." The power of the old Western European citadels had been irreparably broken.

The banker's poem is widely considered one of the best poems in the English language in the last 100 years. The poem met with rapid success and popularity. The poem had been able to articulate the sense of deep loss and despair widely felt at the time.

The poet, T. S. Eliot, launched his career with this poem, "The Wasteland." Eliot despised the Versailles Treaty and he was not alone, many of the great public intellectuals of the time felt the same way. It was a mistake to make Germany the victim; to blame Germany for everything that had gone wrong. With the blame went a crippling debt, a debt Germany's enemies needed it to pay, because they owed a terrific amount in turn to Morgan. Someone must pay for all the blood and loss of economic capital, and with it all the political power that bled from the hands of the Western European Empires.

Eliot and his fellow Harvard alumnus, and close friend of Solomon Trone, Thomas Nelson Perkins felt the same way about the Treaty of Versailles. Perkins had also done the numbers and was well aware that Germany could not pay and knew it. The German negotiators understood when they signed the Treaty that specified the debt as part of Germany's war guilt reparations. If they could not pay and the allies needed the money, the agreement itself was a suicide pact. The allies were tying their economies to an economy that was literally on the edge of complete collapse. When the financial markets would finally see that Germany would default on the reparations then France and England would effectively be in default as well to the financial markets of New York, principally the Banking House of Morgan.

Morgan would eventually send Thomas Nelson Perkins on his final errand, an errand that surely contributed to his declining health. Perkins was faced with the impossible, and of course he failed, because it was impossible.

When Germany did default the allies brought in Morgan to deal with the Germans directly, after all he was really the person behind the Versailles Treaty. Morgan, although his status as the wealth behind the war was politically unofficial, set the terms for the negotiations. Morgan brought in his best representative legal councils Owen D. Young and more importantly Thomas Nelson Perkins.

The deal came down to Perkins. At what point could the Germans not only agree to pay, but actually could pay. Perkins knew the impossibility of the situation. A lovely but seemingly naïve letter from Solomon Trone to Perkins exists from this time. Trone suggests to Perkins that loans can be transferred to other hands than Morgan. Morgan's loans could be bought up by a mass subscription throughout Europe and America.

This way Morgan would get all his money back and Western Europe would have its debt owned by the broad mass of its society. This would make everyone happy so Trone thought. Morgan got his money and Western Europe was free to rebuild outside of the control of Morgan. To this Perkins politely declined. Morgan still wanted his control even if it meant a good deal of loss. Morgan was willing to take that loss. The losses came; roughly half of the war debt was erased by the allies at Perkins' suggestion.

> The debt reduction however was too little too late, and Morgan must have known it. The debt had already started a chain of events that would inevitably lead to war. Western Europe, unwilling to admit it was bankrupt and blinded by a desire for vengeance had forced Germany on to a path that would lead to dictatorship and conflict.

The Blind Allie

The war debt and the indemnity of the reparations debt was widely hated throughout Germany and lead directly to the rise of Hitler and his Nazi Party. The "Stab in the Back" was the rallying cry behind the militarization of Germany and its blind desire for vengeance. Hitler would reap that harvest of discontent finding victims everywhere, from his crazed imagination, to blame the defeat of Germany and the Treaty of Versailles.

General Electric's Clark Haynes Minor was already by this point funneling money to top ranking Nazis through the corporations they owned. General Electric had created alliances with Fascist Europe that ran very deep and were to last until Berlin was occupied by the Soviet Red Army in the spring of 1945[19]. When that happened not surprisingly it would be Solomon Trone who would negotiate secretly between them and Stalin's emissary. But that meeting in war ravaged Berlin was two decades into the future. In the early thirties Solomon Trone knew that the path had been set for a blind march into slaughter. Unable to prevent it, Trone had watched in horror as the West became an armed camp of fear, intolerance and vengeance.

In Mussolini's Italy the power corporation that controlled the power supply was a joint venture between General Electric and the Fascists. Trone was in Rome as an advisor to General Electric International to enhance the power generation systems of Italy, when Mussolini came to power. Later Trone would be in Germany when Hitler came to power, also working as an advisor. As these fascists came to power, General Electric moved to combine and consolidate their operations with those governments. Some of Morgan Banking House were open supporters of Fascism such as Thomas Lamont, who considered himself a propagandist for Fascism in America.

Realizing that he could not continue the relationship with General Electric any more Solomon Trone retired, even though his sudden retirement meant the loss of his pension. He said to his wife that he had to quite before he was found out to be working more for the Revolution than for General Electric. Although he did not go into details, it would have been highly likely that Solomon Trone would have been aware of the deepening connections between the Capitalists in New York City and the European Fascists.

For a time Solomon Trone moved to France. Here he could exist in some degree of freedom. Trone however could not be satisfied unless he knew exactly what was going on. He had already made trips to Germany to keep contact with the German political underground, and had been interrogated by Gestapo. As the situation worsened, Trone desired to know more.

To find out more was the precise reason that Solomon Trone also took a trip to the Soviet Union. To know what was happening in the villages and towns was his mission. He knew that his friends were being eliminated in the planning positions but he hoped officially at least that he might be allowed to live for a time in a village in Siberia. This would never be allowed and perhaps this had only been a ruse by Trone to get into the Soviet Union.

When he came to Moscow he was immediately popular with the social life of the city. He was considered in some reports to be the lion of social society, holding forth with his characteristic stories and jokes. One joke, or rather presumed joke, is that he was there to retire. The Soviet Secret police could not believe what they were hearing and believed this to be part of some deep conspiracy that they did not want to get tangled in.

The Soviet Secret Police or NKVD heard Trone say that he wanted to give up his position as a highly paid consultant with General Electric and become a private citizen in the Soviet Union. To this they had no answer. If he was a Soviet citizen, his conversations would, at that time, have got him executed. The money Trone could make in the West was astronomical to a Soviet person at the time. This fact gave the NKVD deep suspicions as to Trone's motives.

Back in New York Trone sought out his friends on the political left. They were unsympathetic to what he had to tell them about the Soviet Union. While Trone had been away during the last decade, positions on the right and the left had hardened, leaving little room for political independence.

New York had been fertile ground for the independent left of the world, who often found exiles in that city. But this was a very different New York in the early thirties.

When Trone had left a decade before, the round ups of radicals had eliminated many of the top leadership of the radical left. Getting rid of them had involved a combination of imprisonment, torture, exile and executions. Two of the most famous executions were by Electric Chair in Sing-Sing prison in New York State. These people were Fernando Nicola Sacco and Bartolomeo Vanzetti. These anarchists were condemned after an irregular trial by a judge who had vowed he would kill those "Anarchist Bastards."

The Soviet Union had sent their best organizer and propaganda expert, who was also a good friend of Solomon Trone. It was hoped he could help Sacco and Vanzetti escape execution, while at the same time bring more of the political left into the Soviet controlled Communist Party. That organizer was Willie Munzenberg (picture right). This worked to a large degree. Munzenberg was able to build organizations that interlinked with the Communist Party and provided support to left wing causes and these groups that in turn would lend support to the Soviet Union. These

interlocking mutual assistance alliances led directly to a situation where Solomon Trone did not find a friendly ear in New York amongst the political left.

Trone became very depressed at this time, finding virtually no one to talk to. Everywhere in Europe and America two hostile camps were forming. They were being led by fear and anger, and they were rapidly industrializing and arming. Minds were closing and the battle lines were being drawn for an almighty clash that Solomon Trone rightly feared would provide a slaughter that would be on such a scale that nothing could compare.

Endnotes

1	(Ilf and Petrov 1937, 57)
2	(Ilf and Petrov 1937, 57)
3	(Engerman 1997)
4	(Engerman 1997)
5	(Simms 1982)
6	(Kuromiya June 2008)
7	(Kuromiya June 2008)
8	(Loth 1958, 185)
9	(Corporation Reports 1929)
10	(Temin November, 1991)
11	(K. E. Bailes 1974)
12	(Trone, et al. 2009)
13	(Temin November, 1991)
14	(S. Trone, State Department Solomon Trone Interview 1933)
15	(Federal Bureau of Investigations January 12, 1951)
16	(S. Trone, On the Volga, Letters to the Editor 1934)
17	(Federal Bureau of Investigations January 12, 1951)
18	(S. Trone, Correspondence from Trone to Swope 1939)
19	(Flaningam 1945); (United Electrical, Radio and Machine Workers of America 2003)

Chapter 5

VOYAGE OF DISCOVERY

Politics Gets Personal

In 1932 Trone and his new wife Florence decided to voyage into parts unknown and areas of the world they did not think anyone would know them. To make the journey a little more hidden they booked their passage not on passenger ships at all, but on freight ships. The freight ships were going neither to places of cultural significance or to comfortable holiday destinations. This was not a holiday of escape Solomon Trone claimed, despite its anonymity; it was a journey of discovery.

Throughout Trone's life his frequent journey's were directed by political or employment obligations. Because of this he traveled from centers of political and financial power to places of great industrial projects, the largest on earth. This journey in 1932 was to be something different. It was a journey into areas of the globe that were as yet not politically significant, nor particularly valuable for their industrial activity. They were on a journey of un-development, to places of slight political or financial interest, where there was little or nothing happening except life relatively untouched by economic planning.

Why did the Trones do this? The answer is not easy to come to; all we have is his words and the bare facts of a man and woman moving almost anonymously from freight ship to freight ship, in ports on the edges of modern global society. Was he deliberately hiding his whereabouts? Did Solomon Trone know where he wanted to go? Was this merely an excuse for a honeymoon with his new wife? If it was a journey of discovery, what did he wish to discover?

Solomon Trone said he was looking for the causes of unrest. Perhaps the cause of unrest was not these countries, but within himself. A number of events had occurred since he signed the official agreement between the Soviet government and General Electric in 1928. In that agreement what had already been a little known joint development project, became an official agreement recognized by the world in general. Since at that point Solomon Trone had witnessed a definite narrowing of his life. He had also been left a widower in the 1920s, as his wife had died of tuberculosis.

As we have already seen Solomon Trone had just witnessed many events that made him depressed. At this point in the early thirties he had seen at very close range the development of Stalin's terror, the rise of Fascism and the growing intolerance in the West. The world was becoming more and more hostile to independent thinkers who did not want to fit into one opposing camp or the other. While all this was bad, his worst shock came from the death of his closest friend Victor Podpali at the beginning of 1931[1].

Victor died in at a training facility for Soviet foreign agents. This was a place where people learned the necessary skills to be sent out of the Soviet Union and be its agents in other countries. Some have called it a school for spies, but it had very broad function for the foreign policy of the Soviet Union. Victor had died of natural causes, so Solomon was told. As an old political radical he was in the prime target for Stalin's purges. Stalin wanted to get rid of the old guard, as they had proved too independent of his leadership.

Solomon Trone received a document that is the "Political Last Will and Testament of Victor Podpali"[2]. This was a document that Solomon Trone was to keep with him for the rest of his life. It was a treasured document that had only one rival, that of his signed picture of Charles Proteus Steinmentz. Did Victor die as a political victim of the purge? One FBI informant said he had heard Trone say his best friend had been murdered by Stalin. That could only have been Victor Podpali. Informants though are not always correct, and it is possible that statement though accurate was recorded incorrectly. Even innocent deaths appear as sinister in such a time. Regardless of whether it was or was not murder, the loss for Solomon was great. No matter what happened after that point, Solomon would keep the Last Will and Testament with him unless to do so would have put his life or the lives of others in danger.

The Last Will and Testament seems a little strange and embarrassing now. It declares to Trone that his friend Victor would like to be able to die many deaths for the Soviet Union. This is a highly original document, in all my research I cannot find a similar document anywhere. To whatever cause Solomon and Victor had committed themselves in their youth, it had transformed them and guided them. Their commitment to the cause was a commitment to each other. It was an intense comradeship of two who would believe that the highest ideals were possible in each other. Neither had given up the cause, they believed in those ideals within each and that made those ideals real.

Solomon would always have five carnations every year on the anniversary of the Bloody Sunday massacre in 1905. Carnations in Russia are a symbol of that 1905 Uprising, and to Trone they were a symbol of his commitment to the ideals he shared with the comrades who had died. To Solomon Trone there was a commitment to a world that yet did not exist, a world of rational, humane development. The life of Solomon Trone however was filled with losses, losses that followed him in the shape of bitter memories. As long as he remained focused on the enlightenment ideals of his youth, those ideals he shared with Victor and others, then he was strong. His inordinate ability to outface situations where the days were filled with deadly and cheerless confrontations with the reality of evil was one of the most remarkable characteristics of Trone.

Everywhere in 1932 Trone was facing a world turning its back on his values, seeking primitive ideals of dominance, control and the accumulation of power as the only way forward. Trone conversely had the ideal of independent thought as the ultimate goal of man, not power for the sake of power. The important thing for Trone was the rational control of nature, of the world. Planning was not just a device for making the world run on time, it was the ability to decide rationally with consensus and dialogue what we want as a society.

As we shall see later, Trone was often accused of taking everyone else's ideas and having none of his own. This is not entirely incorrect, and for the most part this is what his career entailed. He went out and talked to people informally, he got to know everything about them and their community and the industry. His knowledge of geology, biology, history and economics taught him to know the environment where people lived. Whenever he could he went back to the universities to get more degrees, to listen to lectures and gain as much understanding of science and human society as he could.

The most important task for Solomon Trone was to soak it all in, to simply listen, to learn as much about everything as he could. He would then put these realities, these ideas, these hopes and desires into a plan so that hunger would be erased by the abundance of food, poverty was transformed into wealth, and hope became reality. This was not a process of imposing himself on the world; it was all about getting a picture of the world, with its many facets and many voices, and creating a harmonious progression of these elements into the future. Where there was discord he would try to offer a re-arrangement agreeable to all and conducive to the circumstances so that there would be complimentary collusion of interests and society could move forward to do whatever it wanted to do.

Solomon Trone was nothing by himself, to himself he was but one part that connects so much more. In 1932 Solomon Trone had simply run out of people to talk to, and that to him was a very serious problem. For this reason he traveled to exactly the places he had never been to talk to people he had never met before. He travelled to numerous countries but his main stops were the Philippines, Indonesia, India and Egypt[3]. These were and are some of the most populous countries on earth; they were also countries that were largely non-industrialized at the time.

As the Trones exited from their conspicuous social life in Moscow, New York and Berlin, the legend of Solomon Trone was starting to grow. As Solomon Trone traveled around the world as inconspicuously as he could, he would become more and more of interest to governments who were trying to track his movements.

As report upon report was collected by intelligence agencies the world over the life of Solomon Trone seemed to become more and more into an exotic fantasy about a man who could and should not in reality exist. Many a Secret Service agent then and since would not believe what they were seeing. The reports were contradictory and sometimes cancelled each other out, but as they were collected together a curious picture started to emerge. To some he was working closely with the U.S. State Department and the large American commercial interests, to others he was a close comrade of Lenin and Trotsky[4]. Trone seemed to be everywhere, moving from country to country, always at the center of great political events and shadowed by political intrigue.

Some of these reports ended up on the desk of Ruth Bielaski Shipley, the head of the Passport Division of the State Department. She was a woman of immense power and ability. Though unelected she would hold extraordinary power over the U.S. government that was unchallenged for over 30 years. President Franklin D. Roosevelt would describe as the "wonderful ogre." Her own double life was full of intrigue and political conspiracy, but to the American public she was the image of conservative America.

She held power over Americans in a way that neither before nor after has been repeated. She decided if an American could travel outside of its borders and even deprived Americans of their citizenship. By the time she retired she had personally collected files containing detailed personal information on 12 million Americans, millions of whom had raised her suspicions. Every passport and application, millions upon millions, were carefully scrutinized by her and judged by her peculiar criteria, criteria often not shared by the elected government. She did not need a valid reason to exercise her power; her actions were often extra-constitutional[5].

Although forces in U.S. security apparatus were gathering that would seek to capture Trone, none of those elements would succeed. In the end it would be the powers of Mrs. Shipley in the passport office that would complete this task.

Strange News Indeed

There was no kinder or more genteel Ambassador born than Mr. William Warwick Corcoran, so many people thought. He was certainly brave and generous, few men could match his desire to do the right thing and do it with style. Once in the south of France he had thrown off his fine clothes and plunged into the Mediterranean Sea saving a dozen people from drowning. It was with such panache that he accomplished this act of heroism that he was hailed as a great hero by the French press[6].

Starting life as an adventurous Washington D.C. socialite he squandered his inheritance by the age of thirty. This was a difficult feat to achieve considering his father was a highly influential banker and political lobbyist whom J. P. Morgan Jr. had described as "my venerable friend"[7]. With the loss of wealth and the outbreak of the First World War Corcoran joined the French Foreign Legion. After the war he joined the U.S. Foreign Service in 1920.

In years to come Ambassador Corcoran would save the lives of thousands by engaging in dangerous espionage deep in Nazi territory while he was the Ambassador to Sweden during the war. Entirely on his own without government support of any type he went and found out the pinpoint location of the laboratory, factory and launch site of Nazi Germany's V-2 rocket bases at Peenemunde. Thanks to his bravery the base was bombed and thousands of lives saved. His numerous other espionage exploits would get him the unofficial title of, "The best one man espionage operation in the war."

He would be honoured greatly also for his humanitarian work for Jews that had made it to Sweden and were in need of help. After the war he was able to help the allies track down members of the Nazi high command that had escaped capture.

Corcoran knew bravery and acting on moral principle were the basis of character, but to him of equal importance was a refined sense of propriety and good manners. This meant to Corcoran, among other things, being kind and affable in conversation. Once he punched out a gangster named "The Baltimore Kid," merely because he had made a crude and insulting remark in the presence of a lady. Corcoran could forgive everything but bad manners, and he would risk everything on points of principle and good taste[8].

In Jamaica in December 1933 Corcoran was enjoying one of the few quiet moments in his life. Here in Jamaica as the Ambassador, a position of high social distinction, he had met, courted and married his beautiful wife Dulcie Wylford Parson. It was a time of great joy in Corcoran's life, with nothing to worry about and little to do except be charming.

It was at this point in his life he little expected to experience the strange events of the evening of December 3rd. In had come a delegation of Jamaican and American businessmen who were also the loyal followers of the exiled Black Consciousness leader Marcus Garvey.

It was an unexpected visit. One of the few distasteful aspects of Corcoran's work was to keep a close eye on these possible enemies of the U.S. government, namely Marcus Garvey and his followers. To suddenly have these people show up at his door telling him of threats to the U.S., it seemed a little strange. Corcoran was charm itself. He invited them in, late though the hour was. He tried the best he could to calm the gentlemen down, it was after all the important work of the ambassador to make everyone feel at ease. He offered them drinks, and asked them to tell him their dire news.

As a good host Corcoran listened politely and said nothing to disparage their beliefs and accusations. Somehow or other it appeared to Corcoran their leader, Marcus Garvey had been gravely insulted by a gentlemen who was staying in Jamaica. The man he knew, although he could not imagine what the delegation of businessmen were saying was true about him. He could not imagine it in the least. Corcoran of course did not let on that he thought the whole idea of what they were saying was preposterous[9].

They were saying that a Dr. Solomon Trone who was visiting the island was a Soviet agent.

At some point in Trone's travels he had got to Jamaica, just in time for his wife to give birth to their daughter Vera Alexandra Trone. Her name was derived from the two women in Trone's life that had guided him on his political career. Vera came from the political heroine Vera Figner and

Alexandra was from the lover who had died in his arms in the massacre of Bloody Sunday in 1905.

After the child was born, the Trones had decided to spend the first few months of their daughter's life in Jamaica. Soon after the birth Solomon Trone had made contact with Marcus Garvey. Garvey a gracious host had asked Trone to dine with him. Trone had done so on December 3rd. It had been a raucous event, a debate the likes of which they had not seen in a long time. The debate was one in which Garvey was assailed constantly by Trone, in his desire to enlist the Back to Africa consciousness movement into the global political change promoted by the Soviet Union.

When Corcoran sat there listening at a very late hour to the business leaders, he was somewhat surprised. Corcoran felt deeply sorry for Garvey. He believed Garvey an extremely sincere and generous man, with a refined sensibility like his own, and like himself an ability to spend more than he actually had. He found his pity for Garvey growing as he saw these men imagining Dr. Trone as a Soviet Agent. Such followers, to such a great and sad man, to Corcoran must have seemed so disheartening.

Corcoran had been talking to Dr. Trone on a daily basis since he had landed. Quite apart from his eccentric mannerisms, he was always a jovial and talkative fellow. There was no sign in Trone of the political radical, just a little given to talking about industrial development to such a degree he found unnecessary. But Dr. Trone was not a bore; he merely was an old retired engineer, who perhaps with an absent mind talked a little too much about his profession.

Were the business men right about Dr. Trone being a Soviet agent? In his report to the State Department Corcoran said no, this was no Soviet agent. Dr. Trone had merely talked about his sympathies with the great industrial development projects, something quite natural for an engineer who had worked so long as an executive of General Electric. The followers of Marcus Garvey had merely mistaken idle opinion for something far different and not to be contemplated of the old gentleman.

The statement by Corcoran, though aimed to exonerate Trone, had the opposite effect. It would eventually start a new series of investigations into the life of Dr. Trone. Back in Washington, in the old civil war prison and interrogation center, that was now the Passport Office Mrs. Shipley would read a copy of the report on Trone and put the report in her file on him, waiting for a moment when it could be used. As incredible as it may seem there was little notice taken by the head of the FBI, J. Edgar Hoover at this time.

What had happened was that Trone was now ready to be investigated by many government intelligence organizations in the United States. All Trone had to do was apply for a government position, at which point the letter of slight importance by Corcoran would raise questions that would open a wider investigation that would unleash agents all over the world to find and investigate Dr. Trone.

That trigger would not come for another ten years. In that time Trone would become a major character in an important twentieth century Russian novel, save hundreds from the Nazi concentration camps and help design a plan for the rebirth of China.

Hail to the Technate!

The United States, to which Solomon Trone had entered in 1912, was a very different place to the one he left in 1932. A revolution had taken place in industry, politics and society. Nothing could seem more apparent to this than the great shift in events in national politics and social progress. Yesterday's radicals were today's leaders; the great truths of modern life all began as heresies in a time now long gone in the public mind.

In 1917 a group of American Radicals had met to contemplate overthrowing democracy and instituting something, they considered, much more effective – rule by experts, the managerial elite, those who understood the new technology of the age. These were not minor figures, and their conspiracy to overthrow the constitution of the United States would not find prison cells and executions for their crime of high treason. These people would go on to the highest positions of authority in the United States. This was not even a secret society, their intentions were clear and supported by powerful interests.

They were called the "Technical Alliance." Over half were connected with General Electric in one capacity or another. Their leading members were C. P. Steinmetz and the radical economist Thorstein Veblen (picture right). They imagined a world where the key decisions were not made by elected officials, but experts. The operations of industry and life were to be coordinated by a "Technate" or council of experts and guardians who

would organize society so that every aspect as far as it was possible of social and industrial life would be in harmony.

The theoretical mastermind, Veblen, saw the normal use of political and economic power in society as the ability of primitive barbaric people to sabotage the interests of the community. He and his followers wanted an end to the normal political and economic uses of power in the hands of these social degenerates, even if they were democratically elected officials. Power must be invested in the guardians, the technical elite who would control society through the operations of the "Technate."

The group itself was made up of planning experts from a variety of backgrounds, including forestry, medicine and education. The one woman on the original committee of sixteen was the expert on education. Her name was Alice Barrows Fernandez. Her work for the U.S. Office of Education was in developing and promoting a "platoon school" approach that advocated, what some would consider, a highly a left wing and radical agenda.

Children would develop themselves outside of the usual structured approach to academic subjects. She wanted to give the child a sense of humanism and democratic development by encouraging an individualist approach. She also argued for an emphasis on instilling the importance of technical innovations. She wanted each child to see the importance of technology, by positioning an electric generator so that it would be seen by all students when they entered and exited a school. All students would be made aware, every day, of the functional and operational reality of technology. It was also meant to symbolize the social interdependence of humanity with technology. Technology was not just useful to these Technocrats it was the essence of life, an article of social veneration.

As crazed and this may sound today, at the time this constituted a revolution in thinking. It was a side step away from the old antagonisms in the world of politics. Most issues were not issues at all, with technology there was no issues to be resolved only problems to be fix by trained experts. Where before there was dead lock and contention now there was harmony. Technology, so they argued, gave people a mammoth leap in power and with it the ability to live better with more. The people in this group would hold influential positions in the U.S. Government and some would affect changes to Federal legislation from Coolidge to Nixon. These were not considered crazy at the time and some of their ideas have become common elements in the lives of people all over the world.

One person who was particularly influential was Stuart Chase (picture right). In such books as *Men and Machines* in 1929 (see illustration from the book, right) Chase advocated a world where power and industry was controlled by experts. Chase was considered by Veblen to be the person who most closely under-stood his political economic concepts such as "Sabotage." Chase would advocate numerous causes such as consumer protection, industrial safety and international cooperation. Chase would be extremely successful in pushing forward his agenda for almost half a century. Richard Nixon paid homage to Chase when instituting his laws protecting buyers from unscrupulous advertisers.

Solomon Trone of course knew most of these people socially and often went to the same parties as they did. These were not eccentrics but some of the most learned and respected officials in the United States. Most importantly these people mostly represented the interests of General Electric. The ideal of the Technate and the council of technocrats who stood in power over the rest of mankind were entirely dependent upon the use of General Electric products and the interconnection of Morgan's other industries. The massive restructuring of power and transportation systems was dependent upon purchasing the massive hydro-electric turbines created in mass quantities by General Electric. The Technical Alliance itself was in essence an advertisement strategy for promoting GE products.

With the use of GE products you could remake an entire continent. A continental plan was outlined by the Technocrats that would subordinate almost all aspects of social and industrial life. Long term central and continental planning mirrored in some cases on a one to one basis the Electrification program of the Soviet Union outlined by Lenin. Reading through the plans today side by side with the great Five Year Plans of the Soviet Union, one gets a chilling feeling that this historical synchronicity could not have been an accident.

That we now know that GE had a paid official advising the Bolsheviks from 1917 onward, it does leave one wondering. Was the Soviet Union merely created out of a failed advertising gimmick of General Electric executives? The Technical Alliance plans were hatched in the winter of 1918. These plans predate Lenin's 1920 Electrification program and the 1928

First Five Year Plan. Steinmentz himself reviewed and approved of Lenin's plan. Lenin and Steinmetz liked each other so much they exchanged portrait photos. Steinmentz was on the board of directors for numerous industrial joint projects of Americans and Soviets to develop the Soviet Union. The Technical Alliance and Soviet connection ran very deep.

The plans created by the Technical Alliance were rejected out of hand by politicians in the United States government however. It was too expensive and would require the enforced labour of millions. The problem failed on the most basic level, it was not practical to do such a large scale change. The population itself was nowhere near comfortable entrusting so much power to so few, effectively enslaving a vast majority of the population to great industrial projects. No politician could advocate such a bold and questionable move, not at least at that time. It was also not lost on the politicians that such a move would limit their own authority. When some of these planning elements did see reality in the United States it would be under a different and more democratic method.

It is interesting to note also that the plans included Canada as part of the eventual area of Technate control. Without Canada it was reasoned the power and resources would not be available to truly liberate the productive capacity of the United States. It is also interesting to note that there was not a single Canadian member part of the original Technical Alliance planning committee. The compliance of Canada to hand over its resources was not an issue they considered.

Solomon Trone would see many of these planning ideas implemented in the Soviet Union and in other countries throughout the world. Trone would also see the mistakes that inevitably were created in this way. In the early thirties the entire world seemed enamoured of these grand technical plans based on the original Technate model. As country after country embraced the Technocratic ideal, modified in one way or another, Solomon Trone would become increasingly needed for his skill and experience in making these ideals a reality. Starting from the early thirties Trone would increasingly volunteer as an advisor to many countries, developed and undeveloped, in helping them initiate large scale technical planning.

What had started out as a radical idea in America had become a reality in the Soviet Union, and now with the help of Solomon Trone and the other planners such as Stuart Chase these ideas were spreading like a wild fire throughout the world. Veblen's apostles were taking the world by storm, as country after country adopted national industrial planning to one degree or another.

Of course the main idea behind the Technical Alliance is the massive accumulation of power into one command center that supposedly would be controlled by the technical elite for the betterment of man. This Brain Trust would be the philosopher kings described by Socrates. They would be the elect, but not necessarily elected. They would be wise and humane and be given all the power possible to make the world a better place. What could possibly go wrong with such an idea? By the end of his life, Solomon Trone, although still a true believer in the Brain Trust idea on principle, and an unwavering strong advocate of technocratic revolution, he was more than a little aware of its defects and not particularly sure how to correct them.

One such defect came from an odd source and was to leave Solomon Trone with no recourse left to him but retreat. The women political opponents in Solomon's life would leave him helpless and completely in their power. Trone would meet the one political movement that proved more able to control events than him; this would be the Women's Movement. This group would also prove the best example of why the Technocratic ideal had insurmountable limitations.

A Revolution of One's Own

In 1915, on his back in India after helping Swope in Europe, Solomon Trone would have been forgiven for not knowing about one of the most important political events of the Twentieth Century, which was happening at that very moment. Trone was sick, terribly sick. He had voyaged to Europe with Swope, helped Swope, presumably set up shop in Zurich, while Lenin set up his headquarters in the same city. Then Trone had gone on a long voyage back to America via Goa and Shanghai. In both places Trone was to under orders to familiarize himself with GE operations.

In India he became terribly ill, lost weight and became delusional. This was a usual occurrence when Trone was seriously ill. His highly logical mind, would give way, and his focus would fade. He would see all the things he wanted to ignore, all the events that were distasteful, all the suffering. His voyage out of his safe New York home had landed him near death in India.

In India in 1915, he became seriously ill and languished between life and death and had no reason to live except for the comfort of good conversation in New York if he survived.

In Goa and Mumbai Trone had found little conversation amongst the GE affiliates. He wanted to venture out to the interior, to go to Calcutta,

the center of political radicalism in India. In all probability Trone would have been intent upon seeing the
India's radical political leaders. Of particular interest
would be the expatriate Annie Besant (picture right in
1880s).

Annie was just about to begin her Home Rule campaign for the Freedom of India from the British Empire.
Earlier she had been friends with Karl Marx's daughter Eleanor and had successfully organized numerous
strikes amongst the homeless workers of London, of which she had been
one. She was also a revolutionary determined to overthrow imperialism.
She moved to India absorbing herself into the life of the country. She
would translate the sacred texts of Hinduism from Sanskrit. For the first
time many Hindus in India were able to read their sacred texts because of
her. It was from her translation that the low caste Mahatma Gandhi read
those classics, and was inspired by its ideals. She eventually emerged as
one of India's leaders determined by either weapons or words to drive the
British Imperial armies out of India. Meeting her, Trone knew, would be
indispensable to connecting with the radical movements in India.

To get there however Trone would have to travel over land without the
help of General Electric. To do so, Trone would do what he loved; getting
amongst the people outside of the first class cabin and talking to people
of all classes, finding out as much as he could while he travelled. Such a
strategy occasionally had its drawbacks. This was one occasion where that
strategy had almost proved fatal. While traveling he had become seriously
ill. Trone's political connection with India would have to wait almost half
a century when he would live as a guest in the home of the Prime Minister
of India.

In 1915 however, while Trone writhed in agony, delusional, talking to
dead comrades or imaging prison cells and barricades he had known, the
life of the world was turning around a very important corner. It was an
event that would have important indirect effect on the life of Trone.

In 1915 a delegation of women met at the Hague Belgium to put an
end to the First World War. This was a conference that was heavily represented by American women activists. The bloody slaughter of the war
had just begun, but it was their aim to stop the madness and declare peace
without victory.

Women, as the moral heart of the family should have some control
in the life of the community. They were morally disposed to bring peace

and harmony to the world, so their argument went. Only when they were heard would the heart of world in conflict be satisfied. They had a platform and a number of points that demanded in essence peace be declared immediately and forever.

The first item on the agenda at the Women's International League for Peace and Freedom (WILPF) was not timid and went straight to the point. "We women, in International Congress assembled, protest against the madness and the horror of war, involving as it does a reckless sacrifice of human life and the destruction of so much that humanity has laboured through centuries to build up.[10]"

The further items on the list covered from the decidedly practical to broadly philosophical; there was one however that would have some irony in years to come. Point number nine said, "The Enfranchisement of Women: Since the combined influence of the women of all countries is one of the strongest forces for the prevention of war, and since women can only have full responsibility and effective influence when they have equal rights with men, this International Congress of Women demands their political enfranchisement[11]."

This was a political demand that would be fulfilled largely in the West in the aftermath the First World War. Why this would happen was because of a combination of pressures. Some had opted for extreme political activism as we have seen with Emma Goldman, who was willing to go to prison for the cause, and at the same time some women in high places were able to intervene with significant political influence at the right moment. The combination would eventually get the desired effect, but not before the struggle had undergone some serious trials.

At Hull House the aging Jane Addams was confronted by the young and somewhat aristocratic Alice Paul. The banner of the women's suffrage movement had been held high by Jane, and she was to many the foremost spokeswoman for the cause. She saw something in Alice, one of her long time admirers, which made her relinquish that leadership role. That one thing was power, Alice had it and she knew how to use it. She was also determined to win or die trying. The latter was something that almost came true.

Soon after their meeting Alice Paul would be arrested. This would be a mistake the government would regret. Having been imprisoned and undergone brutal beatings at the hands of the police, Alice Paul had emerged stronger personally and politically. To have working class immigrant girls like Emma Goldman beaten by the police, was perhaps permitted. However for a member of the elite to be stripped naked and have her head smashed against a prison wall until she lay bleeding and unconscious, that was something entirely unacceptable. There was outrage amongst the wealthiest and most politically powerful families in America. Alice Paul had won precisely because she had refused to give in.

The President met her on her release from prison and before long the triumph of women's suffrage in the United States had been accomplished. The politicians claimed that votes for women were part of the war effort. The fact that "votes for women" was an anti-war campaign was neatly brushed aside. The votes for women campaign quickly saw victory because of the war and the activists' determination. But to Alice Paul this was not the end of the struggle. She needed an equal rights amendment and universal peace before she would quit politics. These were two endeavours that she would never see accomplished.

As women in the West gained the vote, they overwhelmingly, outside of Germany of course, voted for the crippling Germany through the Versailles Treaty. Alice Paul did not feel betrayed by this although she was opposed to the Versailles Treaty. She did however feel the need to draw on some strong alliances. She needed to build a women's peace movement internationally, clearly a peace movement at the national level was too limited. This would take time and more education personally to accomplish. She went back to school and then in the late 1920s she made her move.

She started an organization known as the World Women's Party. This would be the voice and advocate for world peace that she desired. This would continue the pledge made in 1915 at the Hague Belgium by the Women's International League for Peace and Freedom.

Operating out of Geneva Switzerland, Alice Paul needed many American radicals to get passports. Luckily for her, and as an affirmation of her great political acumen, Alice Paul had cultivated the friendship of a very powerful woman, Ruth Bielaski Shipley, the head of the Passport Office[12].

As the head of the passport office Ruth Bielaski Shipley had a grasp of the legal intricacies that regarded passports. Shipley would advise the women how to get around the law, a law that she administered. For the needs of the women's movement and world peace, Shipley was not above some secret conspiracies to flout the law. Thanks to modern bureaucracy where all the lines of authority could be converged and one office could give the final say, Shipley became the untouchable mandarin who would not be challenged. If she said the cause was good, you got a passport, if bad you were denied without the right of repeal. It was her cause of world peace and her ideas about and the Women's Movement that created her own foreign policy that sometimes contradicted that of the U.S. State Department.

When Trone married his thirty years younger bride and immediately sent their requests for passports, stating he was ten years younger than he was, Shipley knew that this was a lie. In the margins of the passport application can be seen Shipley's handwriting, "That's not his age!"

It is possible from this point on that Trone was under suspicion. There was however many reasons why Shipley would make Trone the object of her scorn. It would be hard and pointless to say which one tipped the balance; anyone of a number of Trone's qualities could have got him in trouble with Shipley. What we do know is that her reasons for making Trone her enemy were not directed by any government, agency, or law. Her reasons as we will see were personal and she alone responsible.

Endnotes

1   (Federal Bureau of Investigations January 12, 1951); (Trone, et al. 2009); (Podpali 1931); (Federal Bureau of Investigations August 25, 1950)

2   (Trone, et al. 2009); (Podpali 1931)

3   (Trone, et al. 2009)

4   (Federal Bureau of Investigations November 9, 1917 – November 7, 1920); (Trone, et al. 2009); (Federal Bureau of Investigation 1945)

5   (Stetler 1966)

6   (Boyd 1962, B4)

7   (Goldstein 2007)

8   (Boyd 1962, B4)

9   (The Marcus Garvy and the Universal Negro Improvement Association Papers 1990)

10   (Congress of Women at The Hague 1915)

11   (Congress of Women at The Hague 1915)

12   (Amelia R. Fry; Regional Oral History Office, University of California, Berkeley 2011)

Chapter 6

TRONE'S AMERICA

New Deals and Old Friends

Trone had spent much of 1934 and 1935 involved in helping the Soviet Union establish better trade relations with the United States. Since Trone had returned from his around the world travelling, the Soviet Foreign Minister Litvinov had made contact with Trone. Diplomatic relations between the United States and the USSR were being established, and Litvinov felt the need for Trone's help[1]. Trone had developed a number of relations at this time not only with heads of industrial and banking corporations[2] but also the political elite surrounding President Roosevelt[3].

There is some documentation at this time of Trone advising the State Department on trade on behalf of the Soviets at the request of Litvinov[4]. The argument for Soviet trade at the time of diplomatic relations being established was the Soviet Union would primarily be a counter weight to the rise of the Fascist powers. Japan and Germany represented a serious threat to the United States and needed a strong ally.

Trone, in recognition for his work on behalf of the Soviet Union, was invited on April the 4th 1934 to the opening of the Soviet Embassy in Washington. The opening of the Embassy was the final act necessary to re-establish full diplomatic relations[5]. It was an unusual affair as it marked the end of the Soviet Union's official isolation and ironically the beginning of trade decline with the United States. As a rogue state far more trade had taken place. Trone's efforts to re-establish official relations had the opposite effect of improving trade.

At the opening festivities for the embassy, set in the same building as the old imperial Russian embassy, the Soviet Foreign Minister greeted many of Washington's political elite. Amongst those present were advisors to the newly elected President Roosevelt. These advisors were known as the "Brain Trust," many of whom were technocratic in their approach to problems. Trone did have some acquaintance with a numbers of the "Brain Trust," both socially and professionally[6].

The developments in Washington at this time had moved toward embracing many of the ideas of the Technical Alliance which had promoted these ideas from its inception in 1919. The Technical Alliance was a think tank group of engineers. The Great Depression had hit the U.S. economy hard, and people were willing to try new ideas to re-start the economy. In particular the idea of initiating large scale industrial infrastructure projects was commonly promoted. These initiatives were grouped around Roosevelt's political idea of the "New Deal." The New Deal was a series of measures to restart the economy using central economic planning largely to direct large scale industrial infrastructure projects.

One important project was the hydro-electric project the Boulder Dam. Throughout the United States technical efficiency organizations and projects were also started. One particular organization still in existence and highly successful at the time was the Tennessee Valley Authority (TVA). The TVA attempted to modernize farming and industry in a traditionally impoverished area of the United States. It did this by supplying cheap energy, mechanized farm equipment and technical advice.

Trone at this time became quite familiar with these technocratic projects. He spent much of 1934 and 1935 meeting with those who were engaged in directing the various organizations running these projects. As Trone followed these developments closely he became greatly impressed by how they differed from similar projects in other countries that he had seen. In particular the hydro-electric projects were strikingly different from the ones he had seen and had a hand in developing in the Soviet Union.

Not the least of the differences was that the projects were largely outside of the hands of private capital and were directed by government institutions. Instead of relying on private foreign corporations and forced labour as had occurred in the Soviet Union, the U.S. had achieved its objectives using government directed enterprises and labour free of coercion.

Trone saw Roosevelt's "New Deal" measures to revive the economy in the midst of a depression as the technocratic ideal. To Trone it had all the elements that made central economic planning successful. Roosevelt had gathered around him the best educated and experienced professionals and scientists and drawn from them the skills and ideas necessary to rebuild the economy. These people were politically independent of Roosevelt, and often held widely different ideologies from both the left and the right.

Trone at this time became associated with many of the powerful elite of Roosevelt's government. As Trone moved with ease around the social and political circles of Washington's elite, he was also pushing the idea of establishing full relations and expanding trade with the Soviet Union. Ironically Trone was convinced by this point that Stalin was reversing the ideals of the October Revolution[7]. Everything that Trone believed in was under attack with so many European countries lurching to the far right. The situation with Stalin was bad, but the threat from Fascism appeared to be much worse.

Let There Be Light

In the afternoon around 2 PM, the usual Russian time for a mid-day meal, on October 17, 1934 Solomon Trone was sitting down to lunch with his son Dmitri at a Bavarian restaurant in New York City. Dmitri had just returned from the Soviet Union, where he had been the top representative for General Electric[8]. Dmitri in this position had overseen the massive co-operative ventures such as Dnieprovostroi damn, working closely with the head Soviet Engineer Winter and the head of Soviet industrial development, the Bolshevik leader, Kalinin[9].

Solomon Trone at this time would have advised his son to leave General Electric. Having just left General Electric, Solomon Trone had good reason to believe that staying with the corporation necessarily meant working against the Soviet Union and for Fascism[10]. General Electric was becoming deeply involved with the fascist countries, even running joint corporations with them. Trone must have known about this as the connections were at this point public knowledge.

At some point during the meal Dmitri noticed two men sitting in the restaurant having some difficulty ordering from the menu as their English was rudimentary at best.

Dmitri immediately recognized the two men having trouble with the menu. They were the Soviet comedy writers, Ilya Ilf and Eugene Petrov, who Dmitri had met in Moscow previously. Dmitri went over and greeted them in Russian and introduced his father. After a moment or two Dmitri offered to show them around New York City. This was an offer the writers had received from many people already, so they politely declined the offer.

They were apparently in the United States for a short period of time and were quite busy trying to sort out arrangements. They wanted to drive across the country in order to write a book on the United States when they got back to the Soviet Union. They intended to give the most complete picture they could of the United States to the Russian reading public. The project appealed to Solomon Trone immediately. Trone had spent most of his life explaining Russia to Americans, America to Russians – a book such as the one proposed by Ilf and Petrov could be very useful.

Three days later Solomon Trone invited the two writers to a party. With his wife Florence driving Trone talked to the two writers before they got to the party regarding possible help for them in their project to travel around the United States. The writers then set a date with Trone when they could discuss this matter further. It is possible that they could not discuss the matter at the time as Florence had started to sing in Russian the great patriotic classic song "Stenka Razin" in a very loud high pitched voice.

The party to which Trone had invited them was full of people associated with the Technocratic movement including Stuart Chase. The writers were somewhat overwhelmed by the presence of so many people, especially since it was difficult for them to converse in English. The two writers were very popular and people spent a lot of time talking to them. By the end of the evening both writers were extremely exhausted.

Some days later, on the day Trone and the writers had agreed to meet again, Trone did not arrive. Instead he had mixed up the dates and arrived the next day. At this meeting Trone invited the writers out to see Schenectady and the General Electric headquarters and factory. The writers agreed. By this point they had come to the conclusion that Trone was the stereotype of an absent minded professor, the image of him that appeared later in their comic novel about their journey across America entitled *Little Golden America*.

On the trip to Schenectady once again Florence was driving. Trone had explained he could not drive as he was always thinking about industrial and political problems. As such he would easily drive off the road, into a river or perhaps run the risk of crashing into something. Florence loved to drive and drove very fast if she was able to. On the journey to Schenectady the two writers were given a speech by Trone regarding how man can control his environment, his society, his community and his industry.

As they approached Schenectady Trone reminded Florence that she should not drive so fast. Trone explained to the writers, who were not so accustomed to driving cars, that a car crash in America could be very serious, disabling its occupants or even killing them very easily. Trone of course could supply the writers with the exact figures for automobile casualties and deaths on American roads over the past ten years. While Trone held forth on his political discourse quoting statistics at a tremendous pace, the writers scribbled away notes as much as they could for their upcoming book.

As the group approached Schenectady the writers were surprised to find the lights on the highway were appearing twenty kilometers before they arrived in the city of Schenectady. In a Russian context this was unimaginable, as the wide spread use of the electric light bulbs in homes had only recently been introduced. Such a massive use of the technology merely for the use of lighting the road to Schenectady for such a tremendous distance away seemed quite extraordinary.

Once in the city they were impressed with the massive sign of General Electric written out in light bulbs that appeared as high as a ten story building. Trone had chosen Schenectady and General Electric because this was what America mostly was to him, it's incredibly powerful electrical industry.

Trone wasted no time in taking the writers to see a salesman for GE named Ripley, who used an idealized home built inside GE headquarters to demonstrate the home of the future. Here labour saving technology made life easy, and automation reduced the needed to remember anything. The individual was wrapped in technology and with it comfort.

The house was even designed to be "fool proof," where a fool could live without making a mistake. The concept impressed and even appeared to shock the two writers, "The technology distrusts man, has no faith in his resourcefulness" they wrote. The whole experience seemed like something straight out of the Russian Folk tale where a house becomes alive, due to the spells of a witch.

The two writers put a question to Trone that was perhaps quite obvious. How could ordinary Americans' afford all these highly technical machines? As the Great Depression had made so many unemployed and conditions for many more were much reduced, it seemed strange that such technology could be sold to anyone. This was extreme luxury, an unnecessary excess at the time when basic needs were not being met. Trone let them in on Swope's great idea: Credit.

Trone explained that no one bought anything out right, but put everything on credit. By the time the debt was paid off the machines had to be replaced. New items had to be purchased because the original machines would be worn out and out of date. Forever the American citizen owed everything, owned nothing, and yet could count himself the beneficiary of incredible technical convenience.

The writers could see the obvious dilemma that the credit system promoted by GE presented. What if you lose your job? Then you could not keep up on the payments on the debt. To this there was no obvious answer that could be given.

Also, the writers pointed out, the products were quite reliable and looked as though they would last forever. Why should people buy new ones? Eventually the needs would stop, as everyone eventually would have what they needed; the factories producing the technology would have to close down. To this, Trone pointed out, there was an answer; the American corporation manufactures the need as well as the product to answer the need.

The needs that their products answered were needs you did not know you had. These were needs you would have in the future, that GE was answering today. The advertising campaigns and publicity talked of a future world that was so enticing you wanted it today. The propaganda envisioned a world that you would like to exist, not necessarily what did exist.

The technical innovation was to the Russian writers incredible. No less incredible was the economic system that created this technical innovation. Both were the embodiments of mysterious even mystical processes that would be behind the continuous questions they were to ask, and never fully answer, on their journey across America.

Discovering Trone

The trip to Schenectady convinced the Russian writers that they had found the perfect traveling companions. The Trones were of independent means and therefore did not require payment for their help, they also seemed quite eager to help them on this journey they were planning. The Trones also spoke perfect Russian and English and did not appear to mind acting as translators. The Trones also knew about traveling in the United States, at least one of them could drive and perhaps most importantly Solomon Trone appeared to be well connected and a virtual encyclopedia and warehouse of information on America.

The drawback was that the Trones had a small daughter who was under five years old that they would have to leave behind with a nanny in New York. The two writers felt terrible asking the Trones to go with them, but it did appear to everyone as the best opportunity to produce a successful popular work explaining America to Russians. To Trone it seemed a great opportunity.

The two writers were considered and still are considered literary masters. Whatever they wrote would be immediately read by all of the reading population of the Soviet Union. The ability to help his fellow Russians know America as he knew it was a temptation that Trone could not resist.

Both he and Florence agreed to help the two writers on their journey of discovery across the United States.

Trone would be described in the book as, "A fat little man with a clean-shaven head on which glistened large beads of icy sweat came up to us." The description is quite accurate for Trone, as he did in fact have a short and somewhat large body. He was also described as somewhat of a comic absent minded professor type, who knew everything but had trouble doing the most basic things. He walked into stationary objects, talked incessantly in a particularly curious way and appeared almost Dickensian in his extravagant mannerisms.

To say this was all a true and correct depiction of Trone misses a very important detail. Ilf and Petrov were comic writers, and they wrote comic depictions of people that have a special place Russian cultural memory. Their depiction of Trone is at one and the same time accurate and inaccurate. Everything appears true, and yet it misses so much that would make the characterization less humorous. While Trone was short and squat he was also very physically fit. While Trone appeared to be absent minded, he was always mindful never to give any information regarding his history that might compromise himself or them.

As Florence drove the writers across America, Trone took the drivers on a mental journey to detail and understand in depth the country they were seeing. If the writers did not see how skillfully Trone had planned their journey to develop their understanding, it shows how Trone set out to educate them without appearing to lecture them. Of course the writers were aware that Trone had planned every detail of the trip very quickly. "The itinerary (created by Trone) made our heads go around," they would write. What they did not fully realize was that every item on the itinerary was designed to orchestrate a particular understanding of America that Trone wished the writers to express in their book.

It is one of the great skills of Trone that he knew how to make people feel comfortable and by degrees gain their confidence and eventually lead them to engage with him in trying to understand the world around them. Trone was no fool, but he would always appear open and ready to learn, everyone had something to teach him. As the group made their way across America Trone would engage everyone in conversation, from small children, to hitch hikers, to corporate executives.

Trone was acting as the hunter for knowledge that fed the writers who patiently recorded everything that would be translated to them. Only a fool or a wise man would ask as many questions as Trone did. The foolish old professor appears funnier in print than the relentless discourses of an investigative planning expert. The picture of Trone is only partially given in order to make the book funnier. If the character of Trone, called Mr. Adams in the book, appears as comic in his foolishness, it is not so much an inaccurate representation of his character as it is merely just one way seeing him. The novel is widely considered to be entertaining; the writers gave an accurate but in many ways an incomplete picture of Trone in order to achieve this.

Trone of course was very busy giving an incomplete picture to the writers. Constantly Florence and Trone exchanged looks, silently questioning each other about what was safe to say. If the writers had known how close Trone hand been to the events of 1917 or how well he knew the people who were responsible for the political purges currently underway in the Soviet Union then both Ilf and Petrov may have had second thoughts about working with Trone. There were many subjects that not discussed with the two writers.

Trone was careful to manage the journey from beginning to end so that the writers would get the information and experiences they needed to produce a comprehensive work of literature that would help Russian readers understand America better. As Trone's character in the novel said, "I want to help you. No, no, no! You don't understand. I regard it as my duty to help every Soviet person who comes to America." What better way to help every Soviet person than an easy to read fun guide explaining America from top to bottom, from coast to coast. Trone knew that the best way to understand the country was by traveling across it. "It would be foolish to think that you could find out anything about America by sitting in New York."

Once the Trones had agreed to participate in the trip across America, Trone immediately set to work planning the trip. It is from the writings of Ilf and Petrov that we are given a very privileged view of how Trone worked as an industrial planner. We see Trone taking charge as if the project was of utmost seriousness. An appearance that seems quite comical is given as Trone places great significance to planning what is meant to be a simple light hearted road trip.

> We need a plan! A plan for the journey! That's the main thing! And
> I will make that plan for you. No, no, don't talk! You cannot possi-
> bly know anything about it!" He suddenly took off his coat, pulled
> off his spectacles, flung them on the couch (later he looked for
> them in his pockets for about ten minutes), spread an automobile

road map of America on his lap, and began to trace curious lines on it. Right there before our eyes he was transformed from a wild eccentric into a businesslike American.[11]

Ilf and Petrov despite their attempts to give a Trone a comical character in the person of Mr. Adams, the dual nature of Trone does make an appearance throughout the work. Trone is shown as a romantic and at the same time a professional serious minded planner. Even simple decisions over whether one should travel by one highway or another was analyzed by Trone and using his imagination he would create a dramatic picture where life and death hung in the balance on that seemingly very simple question. "This is very, very dangerous. It would be foolish to risk your lives. No, no, no! You cannot imagine what an automobile journey is[12]."

On the day that the journey began the image Trone presented of himself seemed entirely different. Dressed in his executive clothing, Trone had transformed himself from the romantic absent minded professor into a very diplomatic looking person:

> He was unrecognizable. He was solemn and deliberate. All the buttons of his vest were buttoned. Thus the ambassador of a neighbouring friendly power comes to call on the minister of foreign affairs and declares that the government of his Excellency considers itself now in a state of war with the power the representative of which is the abovementioned minister of foreign affairs[13].

This is probably how Trone would have presented himself on the numerous occasions that he did mix with heads of state. This is hardly the absent minded professor that Ilf and Petrov describe throughout the book. One of the most remarkable aspects to the work by Ilf and Petrov is that despite their efforts to present a two dimensional comic character out of Trone the real more complex character often can be seen in the text. Trone is supposed to be an absent minded professor type, and yet glimpses are given of a very different type of person, with a very unusual and different history that exists beneath the character type described by Ilf and Petrov.

It was shortly after the group left New York that a hint is given of Trone's political ideals:

> "Stop!" Mr. Adams (Trone) suddenly shouted. "You must see it and write it down in your notebooks."
> The machine stopped.

> We saw quite a large yellow bill-board inspired by no mere com-
> mercial idea. Some American philosopher, with the aid of a press
> agency, had placed on the road the following declaration: "Revolu-
> tion is a form of government possible only abroad."
> Mr. Adams (Trone) gloated.
> "No, gentlemen," he said, in his joy forgetting about his hat, "you
> simply don't understand what is advertising in America. The Amer-
> ican is accustomed to believe in advertisements. You must under-
> stand that. Revolution is simply impossible in our country. You are
> told that on a highway as infallible truth by this press agency[14]."

Trone's love for America, its technology, and its people were aspects he wished other Russians could share. These elements were at the heart of who Trone was as a person. Coupled with that deep love for America was a serious caution. America was lost in its illusions, they believe their propaganda to such a degree it was impossible for Russians to at first comprehend it.

The Russia Trone knew is one where the government advertises its actions, gives out its propaganda filled with obvious lies. Whether it was the government by Stalin or by the Czar, whatever was the official government statement, most Russians automatically distrusted it; they had become accustomed to disbelieving what they were told. Official pronouncements, newspapers, and posters gave what you were supposed to believe, but were wrong so often that no ever did believe them.

Trone was trying to explain to Russians an essential truth of America. Its illusions are believed. The advertising works. An American does not automatically disbelieve the propaganda. In America the propaganda is slick, it uses methods perfected to a high degree and it forms an important part of the cultural life of the society. The advertising in America was its cultural backbone, to understand America you had to understand how important its advertising was to the life of the nation.

To illustrate this point Trone would continuously throughout the novel point out differences in American and Russian perception.

> ...do you really think that Ford is famous in America because he
> created a cheap automobile? Oh, no! It would be foolish to think
> that! It is simply because throughout the country automobiles run
> around with his surname on the radiator. With you, Ford the me-
> chanic is famous; with us, Ford the merchant.[15]

To Trone the American interconnection with advertising was not a weakness. The Americans, to Trone were not, gullible fools ready to do anything because they were told to. Trone had to make it clear to Russians; the America he knew was integrated into its advertising, propaganda, mass media and Hollywood culture, not because Americans were deficient but because they respect efficiency above all. "He must be told which god to worship. He cannot decide for himself. Besides, he has no time to make the decision; he is a busy man."[16]

The book serves as Trone's personal speech to Russia, a Russia he wanted to emulate the United States. Now that emulation had taken hold of Russia, partly thanks to him, he wanted to warn Russia about what it was getting itself into. Russia could never be America, but it could learn from America, both the good and the bad.

Trone put his argument quite simply, "It is a purely American characteristic not to do any more than necessary[17]." This was the essence of America both its greatness and its serious defects. As the group visited the industrial centers of America, including the car factories of Detroit, Trone pointed out that much of what was admired in America related to its ability to do everything on a mass scale, relying on simple processes using the maximum amount of automation possible. Where critical judgment, individual skill, taste and intelligence were required, serious deficiencies could be seen. Precisely because American society worked to make everything as efficient as possible on a mass scale, it lost the ability to do processes that required individual expertise on a small scale. Processes that cannot be easily defined and replicated on a mass scale were areas where the U.S. economy simply could not compete.

Trone gave the specific example of professional drawing instruments that were produced in Germany rather than in America:

> We cannot make drawing instruments. Gentlemen, don't laugh! Not that we do not want to; no, we cannot. America with all of its grandiose technique does not know how to manufacture drawing instruments. This is the same America which makes millions of automobiles a year! And do you know where in the trouble lies? If the drawing instruments were needed by the entire population, we would organize mass production and would produce tons of millions of drawing instruments at an amazingly low price. But the population of the United States does not need tons of millions of drawing instruments. It needs only tens of thousands. That means that it is impossible to establish mass production, and drawing instruments would have to be made by hand. And everything which in America is made not by machinery, but by the hand of man,

costs incredibly much. So our drawing instruments would cost ten times more than the German ones. Mr. Ilf and Mr. Petrov, write this down in your little books, that this great America finds itself at times helpless before pathetic old Europe. That is very, very important to know![18]

Where production required either an indiscernible quality that could not be defined or it were only production on a small scale was necessary then the American system of manufacturing fell apart.

The Soviet Union could transplant American methods of economic production, but it was a method with serious deficiencies. The American intoxication with advertising and its inability to do things on a small scale were just two elements that Trone was warning about. Some elements could be transplanted; other aspects were probably too foreign for Russians to embrace. Even if the economy of the United States could be replicated in the Soviet Union, it would bring with it new problems. Broad needs of the population would be answered using American mass production but some products that could not be mass produced may become more difficult to obtain.

Trone throughout the work by Ilf and Petrov appears like a salesman with some feelings of remorse, after a sale of a deficient product. After all his experience he knew that Russia was mistaking America. It had seen what it wanted to see, falling in love with an America that did not exist exactly as they thought it did. Trone wanted Russia to discover the real America, one that was as full of faults as it was full of wonders. Trone wanted Russians to see America as he saw it.

By this point in Trone had spent almost half of his life outside of Russia. He had been employed by General Electric for the majority of his working life. Trone knew America from its most powerful citizens to its most wretched poor. The Trone who had promoted the plan to develop the former Russian Empire on the model of American industry now had serious reservations about the attempt. Trone realized that the complete replication of the American model was neither possible to achieve nor desirable to attempt.

The American model demanded industrial production controlled through credit. As Trone had seen, and Ilf and Petrov had pointed out, the failure to pay could have dire consequences, whether it was for a nation with a foreign loan or an individual who had purchased a car on credit. Related to this was a system that demanded constant technological innovation, regardless of whether it was needed or not to drive sales made possible with the help of credit. To make production low cost and create the desire for purchasing, mass propaganda and advertising were essential. Through the use of mass advertising and propaganda consumer and worker behavior were controlled to an unheard of degree.

These were all elements that Trone and the two Soviet writers recognized as having potentially sinister implications. The American love of efficiency, the desire to make the world simple, brought with it an obvious deficiency, a society too narrow and simplistic for man to develop. It had the potential to be a society that could be reduced to a limited number of objectives set by large corporate centers where power had been concentrated. Life had the potential to be reduced to the bland, and the overly controlled.

America was a place where the mass needs of society had been met, it was a wonderful leap forward from Czarist Russia, where no one was educated, starvation was common, and life expectancy did not rise much above 30. Here there was mass production, providing all that was necessary for raising the standard of living and increasing the life expectancy to levels that to Russians seemed incredible. It had its draw backs to be sure, but Trone and the writers had to admit by comparison to other countries, it was a definite step forward for humanity.

One day on the journey Ilf and Petrov decided to take a quick look across the border into Mexico. In Mexico the writers found many of the deficiencies that are common outside of the industrialized world. Returning back they both expressed relief to Trone about being in the U.S. again. Trone used the opportunity to drive home his oft repeated message about America:

> I want to tell you that this is a country where you can calmly drink raw water out of a tap without catching typhoid fever – the water will always be perfect. This is a country you need never look suspiciously at the linen in your hotel, for the linen will always be clean. This is a country where you don't have to think of how to drive by automobile from one city to another. The road will always be good. This is a country where in the cheapest restaurant you will not be poisoned. The food may not be to your taste, but it will always be of good quality. This is a country with a high standard of living. And this becomes especially clear, gentlemen, when you happen, as we did today, to visit another American country. No I don't mean to say that the United States is a remarkable country but it has its attributes and you must always remember that[19].

Despite America's blandness, its efficiency taken to an absurd level and its lack of critical thought, it had the singular advantage of providing adequately for the basic needs of life. Its water was safe, its food was plentiful and all the amenities for community life were available.

In the praise and criticism of America, Trone and the Soviet writers were giving a warning to the Russian reader. This is the society from which we are borrowing so much, it has benefits as well as drawbacks. As Ilf and Petrov criticize America, they were by extension criticizing a Russia that was in love with and emulating America. In the book America is both something to be avoided and something to be embraced. Ilf and Petrov expressed this view early in the work:

> We tried to generalize. Scores of times we exclaimed:
> "Americans are as naive as children!"
> "Americans are excellent workers!"
> "Americans are sanctimonious!"
> "Americans are a great nation!"
> "Americans are stingy!"
> "Americans are senselessly generous!"
> "Americans are radical!"
> "Americans are stupid, conservative, hopeless!"
> "There will never be a revolution in America!"
> "There will be a revolution in America within a few days!"[20]

The book by Ilf and Petrov expressed the exact antipathy that Trone felt toward America both as a model for industrial development and as the place where he called home. As the book was an exploration of Trone's view of the world, it was also an in depth exploration of Trone.

Frequently in the book Ilf and Petrov found themselves fascinated by the unique, strange and often inexplicable actions of Trone. Some of the things he knew, such as the date the next war would start, seemed odd with no possible basis in fact. How could a man, who was only an engineer, know all the high policies of state, and when countries were planning to go to war? Trone did not speak in an idle manner, when he spoke he spoke of certainties and scientific facts. His pronouncements were presented as if there were no other point of view possible. As the book progresses a different person starts to emerge in Mr. Adams the character meant to be Trone. "Mr. Adams was very absent-minded. Yet his was not the traditional meek absent-mindedness of a scientist, but rather the stormy, aggressive absent-mindedness of a healthy person full of curiosity carried away by a conversation or a thought and for the time being forgetting the rest of the world[21]."

Elsewhere the writers speak about Trone background that appears somehow a little more than an average engineer:

> Mr. Adams knew many languages. He had lived in Japan, Russia, Germany, India, knew the Soviet Union well – better than many Soviet people know it. He had worked at Dnieprostroi, in Stalingrad, Chelyabinsk. Knowledge of old Russia made it possible for him to understand the Soviet land as it is rarely understood by foreigners. He had travelled across the U.S.S.R. in hard cars, entered into conversation with workers and collective farmers. He saw the country not only as it opened to his gaze, but he saw it as it had been yesterday and as it would become tomorrow. He saw it in motion, and for that purpose he studied Marx and Lenin, read the speeches of Stalin, and subscribed to Pravda[22].

This was an extraordinary individual. He was extremely knowledgeable about the Soviet Union and was keen to know everything about the politics and development in that country. His level of knowledge was not that of an engineer, but more of a diplomat and a scientist, a politician or a writer. Trone's claim to be a mere technical expert seemed quite a bit short of the mark. Even though the Trone's character of Mr. Adams is used for comic effect, Ilf and Petrov cannot help describing an unusual individual, incredibly talented, unusually experienced and somehow oddly out of place. For an engineer his interests seemed to be broader and more esoteric and philosophical. To be a politician, diplomat, or businessman his knowledge of technical detail seemed excessive.

With Ilf and Petrov's description of Trone, there was something not quite right. The reader of the work must either come to the conclusion that the description is deliberately left incomplete or that Ilf and Petrov did not fully know who they were describing. Considering the literary ability of Ilf and Petrov it seems unlikely that they would make a mistake in giving an incomplete characterization of Trone. It seems more likely that the description is accurate of a man who could not fully reveal who he was.

This deliberate act to obscure who he was does not however limit the power of Ilf and Petrov to analyze the character of Trone. To a great extent the writers capture the spirit of the man without exactly understanding who he was and what he did. A good example of this is contained in their description of Trone's incredibly social character:

> This man was born to mingle with people, to be friends with them. He derived the same pleasure from conversations with a waiter, a druggist, a passer-by from whom he found out about the roads, a six-year-old black boy, whom he called "sir," the mistress of a tourist home, or the director of a large bank[23].

From the characterization given by Ilf and Petrov it is quite clear how Trone was able to be so successful in his work gathering information. The writers describe in some detail at numerous points Trone's unusual ability to listen and get vast amounts of information out of people with only a few words. In a few moments on arriving in a town Trone would have met someone and from that brief encounter he would have learned the financial and social health of the community as well as what recent tragedies and usual events had occurred.

He was a magnate for conversation. To Ilf and Petrov he spoke endlessly to everyone. He listened with absolute attention gathering in information. Trone acted as a means of communication for America to speak to Ilf and Petrov, and by that means for Ilf and Petrov to understand and eventually represent America in their writing.

The Ironic Traveler

The trip went through the state of New York, on to Detroit, Chicago, then swinging south journeying to Los Angeles via Kansas City and Santa Fe. The way back to New York would skirt the Mexican Border, the Gulf of Mexico and then follow the east coast north to New York City. The trip was from October 29th 1935 to January 13th 1936.

Trone had carefully planned out meetings with industrial leaders such as Henry Ford and with great engineers such as the Chief Engineer Thompson of the Boulder Dam project. It was not the original intention of the two writers to see primarily points of industrial interest, as they had gone to great pains to get letters of introduction to great artists and entertainers in the United States.

Trone was able to combine in the trip destinations of industrial, economic and political as well as artistic importance. Unfortunately Trone was less successful at helping the writers meet the great artists such as Charlie Chaplin. In Los Angeles particularly, Trone had virtually no connections. Because of this he left the writers in Los Angeles while he and his wife went to Mexico. Left to their own initiative the two writers sat in a hotel room for weeks without being able to meet with anyone of significance.

In other locations Trone was able to act as a tour guide dispensing information regarding the politics, the economy and even the history of the areas they passed through. Upon entering California, Trone felt it necessary to make a comment. The two writers were awe struck at the luscious vegetation that they were seeing. California appeared like a paradise with incredible gardens and agriculture that they were shocked to see so soon after leaving the desert.

> "Gentlemen," Mr. Adams (Trone) was saying solemnly, "you must remember that all the plants you see here - palms, pines, apple and lemon trees, every blade of grass – have been planted here by the hand of man. California was not at all a paradise; it was a desert. California was made by Water, roads, and electricity. Deprive California of artificial irrigation for one week, and it will be impossible to repair this misfortune for years. It will again become a desert. We call California the Golden State. But it would be more correct to call it the state of man's remarkable labour. In this paradise it is necessary to toil endlessly, uninterruptedly; otherwise it will turn into a hell. Remember that, gentlemen! Water, roads, and electricity![24] "

At every place Trone tried to make comprehensible what was inexplicable to the Russians. Russians so used to a society where scarcity was as much present as abundance was present in the United States, would not be able to comprehend how this situation had occurred. Trone knew the details of its development and wanted very much to help show how step by step America had built itself into what it was. To Trone, this was not magic nor was it primarily a difference in ideology that had created the wonders of America; it was the triumph of scientific technical application over nature. This was the change he wanted for Russia, this was the message he wanted to give Russia through the writings of Ilf and Petrov.

Were Ilf and Petrov converted disciples of Trone's technocratic way of thinking? The answer to that is no, but with some qualification. The commitment to the Soviet Union of the two writers was one of support but they had broader view of humanity and their work than can be contained in a political ideology. Ilf and Petrov are rightly considered two of the greatest Russian writers of the Twentieth century, well known and widely read even today.

Russia has a long tradition of great works of comedy starting with the stories of Nikolai Gogol. The themes of Russian comedy even today often revolve around man's relationship or struggle with the large bureaucratic organizations that are ever present in Russian life. Ilf and Petrov are best remembered for their creation of the anti-hero Ostap Bender whose exploits always include some trick or other to exist as an outsider, free from both the law and societal norms.

When Ilf and Petrov met with Trone they were of course dealing with an extraordinary character in his own right. Trone provided for them a journey with commentary to see a society very different from their own. Trone himself appeared as a strange guide who knew almost everything and yet seemed incapable of doing anything without the assistance of his wife. Comic irony was an essential element in the writings of Ilf and Petrov. The ironic nature of Trone therefore comes out not just in how they look at his character but also his ideas.

Trone is portrayed as a man who admires technical advance merely because it is technical advance. Trone at one point in the journey while they were enjoying a meal at a roadside café, orders a beer:

> Mr. Adams (Trone), who never drank anything, suddenly ordered beer. The young waiter brought two tin-cans, the kind in which we sell green peas. "This is a tremendous business," said Mr. Adams (Trone), watching the waiter open the tin-cans of beer, "and until now no one could make a go of it. The trouble was with the odour of the tin. Beer demands an oaken barrel and glassware, but you must understand, gentlemen, that it is not convenient to transport beer in bottles, besides being too costly. Bottles take up too much room. They add to the excessive expense of transportation.
>
> Recently a lacquer has been perfected which corresponds perfectly to the odour of a beer barrel, if one may say so. By the way, they looked for this lacquer to fill the needs of a certain electric production, and not for the sake of beer. Now they cover with it the inside of tin-cans, and the beer has no foreign taste at all. This is a big business!" He drank two glasses of beer, which he really didn't like at all. He drank it out of respect for technique. The beer was quite good[25].

To Ilf and Petrov the highly focused Trone was perhaps a little too focused. Seen as being unusually careful and conservative, Trone often becomes a source of fun for the writers in his predictability and meticulousness. It is not that they disagreed with Trone, quite the opposite they did agree with his many observations. There is of course more to life than the technical progress to which Trone had dedicated his life.

In many ways what comes through in the text is not the admiration for the great engineer, but a deep and growing sympathy for him. Trone is seen as a highly romantic and kind man who wants genuinely to enjoy the company of others and help where he can. The sympathy for Trone most comes out when Trone appreciates the abilities and the triumphs of others.

A curious and perhaps telling event occurred when the group visited a First Nations Reserve. Trone and the writers spoke first with a non-First Nations person who devoted his time to helping those on the reserve.

> "I wanted to make Christians out of the Indians," the man in the red shirt, with a cartridge belt, told us, "but it didn't turn out as I expected: they made an Indian out of me. Yes! Now I am a real Indian. If you like I'll take your scalp off!" And laughing loudly lie pretended to scalp Mr. Adams (Trone). Then he sat down and, still smiling, added thoughtfully: "And to tell you the truth, I don't know more honest, noble, and clean-cut people than the Indians. They taught me to love the sun, the moon, the desert. They taught me to understand nature. I cannot imagine now how I could live away from the Indians."

"Sir," Mr. Adams said suddenly, "you are a good man." He took out a handkerchief and wiped his eyes, without taking off his eyeglasses[26]."

It is this desire to live for a good cause in harmony with people that is important to the character of Trone described by Ilf and Petrov. When in San Francisco, the writers described a meeting with a small Russian religious sect that had immigrated to the United States.

> Mr. Adams (Trone), who had wiped his eyes several times and was now even more profoundly affected than during his conversation with the former missionary about the manly Navajo Indians, could not contain himself any longer and began to sing in chorus with the Molokans. But here a surprise awaited us. The Molokans introduced their own ideological correction when they came to the words: "The dark clays are over; the hour of deliverance has struck." They sang it thus: "The dark days are over; Christ has shown us the way." Mr. Adams (Trone), the old atheist and materialist, did not make out the words and continued to sing loudly, opening wide his mouth[27]."

Trone did not want to be a Molokan or help out on the reserve but he did want to help build a strong community. Whether in the planning of industrial regions, agricultural colonies or just developing a broad social network of friends, Trone was continuously trying to bring people together in harmony. The great irony of Trone that the writers were able to grasp, without fully knowing who he was, is that this was a man devoted to helping others, to building a stronger, healthier society, was in essence an outsider.

Trone was not a member of any political group, nor did he subscribe to a particular political creed. The one group he disavowed his membership in was the Jewish community, claiming nothing about him was Jewish. Yet, even here a great deal of his life was sacrificed to helping Jewish causes and as we will see he played an important role within the Jewish community.

Trone did not quite fit in anywhere and yet was trying to help the society of man as a whole, not recognizing any division that separated man from man. Trone existed to bring people and societies closer together. Somehow Ilf and Petrov saw this clearly; they portrayed Trone in such a way as to show his incredibly generous nature at the same time as they made clear the profound sense of irony that was central to his character.

Perhaps the book, *Little Golden America*, is the best testament to Trone that can be given. He is not seen as heroic, political or powerful dealing with matters of great importance. Trone is seen as someone who simply likes to enjoy the company of others. He is not a man full of self-possession, convinced of his innate genius and ability to lead. Trone wants to learn from others and just being sociable gives him the greatest pleasure.

Trone was a man of science, an engineer, someone devoted to technique and great industrial projects, but at bottom he was very much a people person. Trone was a man divorced from society on so many levels. Constantly traveling, constantly dealing with technical issues and forever looking for a better way forward politically, Trone led a life that was very unusual. The irony of a man who is so technical, scientific and theoretical but finds his greatest joy in being social was something that Ilf and Petrov saw as integral to the character of Trone

In truth Trone never was a great engineer, nor was he political leader of any kind. He could not be said to be a business man, nor was he great diplomat. Trone enjoyed bringing people, ideas and communities together; that is what he did best and that is what he enjoyed the most.

Trone and the writers became very good friends as a result of the journey. Trone also did not object to any of the characterizations of himself made by Ilf and Petrov. Today the character based on Trone of "Mr. Adams" has joined the cultural landscape of Russia as one of the most amusing characters to be found in Russian literature.

Most academicians, who study *Little Golden America*, usually get stuck when they analyze the character of Mr. Adams. It is commonly stated that Trone and Mr. Adams are radically different people, but this is not true. Ilf and Petrov may have only captured part of Trone's character in print, but it is a very important part, perhaps the most essential.

Another mistake made by scholars is to presume Trone was an agent of Stalin, because of what limited documentation and literature exists that mentions Trone points to this conclusion. Trone however especially at this point was radically anti-Stalin. His love for Russia and the political ideals of 1917 were undiminished, but after the Stalinist show trial he attended, his wife said he was never the same again.

Trone was a man continuously trying to build a better world, he was undaunted by the evil he witnessed but not unaffected by it. Ilf and Petrov portray a man who desperately wants to say something to the Russian people and the world, because he believed that the situation even then was not hopeless, and that something better was possible.

Endnotes

1   (Soviet Envoy Host At Brilliant Fete 1934); (Federal Bureau of Investigations January 12, 1951)
2   (Plans Laid to Trade with Russia 1934)
3   (Federal Bureau of Investigation 1945); (Federal Bureau of Investigation 1949); (Van Kleeck 1935- 1943); (Federal Bureau of Investigation 1953)
4   (Federal Bureau of Investigations January 12, 1951)
5   (Soviet Envoy Host At Brilliant Fete 1934, 14)
6   (Il'f 2000); (Soviet Envoy Host At Brilliant Fete 1934)
7   (Federal Bureau of Investigations 1951)
8   (Il'f 2000)
9   (D. Trone 1978)
10   (Trone, et al. 2009)
11   (Ilf and Petrov 1937, 89)
12   (Ilf and Petrov 1937, 151)
13   (Ilf and Petrov 1937, 55)
14   (Ilf and Petrov 1937, 89)
15   (Ilf and Petrov 1937, 186)
16   (Ilf and Petrov 1937, 240)
17   (Ilf and Petrov 1937, 93)
18   (Ilf and Petrov 1937, 129)
19   (Ilf and Petrov 1937, 260)
20   (Ilf and Petrov 1937, 85)
21   (Ilf and Petrov 1937, 105)
22   (Ilf and Petrov 1937, 105)
23   (Ilf and Petrov 1937, 106)
24   (Ilf and Petrov 1937, 250)
25   (Ilf and Petrov 1937, 121)
26   (Ilf and Petrov 1937, 175)
27   (Ilf and Petrov 1937, 213)

Chapter 7

A SIMPLE MATTER OF PERSPECTIVE

The arc of the moral universe is long but it bends toward justice.
– Theodore Parker, Unitarian minister,
reformer and abolitionist, 1860.

A Point of View

The story of Trone from the winter of 1939 to the summer of 1940 can only be told from the point of view of a suitcase. It is a suitcase that has been stored in a closet for almost seventy years, never opened until now. Of the millions sent down the train tracks to places such as Auschwitz, this suitcase contains thousands of their voices, voices of the condemned. The suitcase had not been opened in all those years since the war. All that time no one felt the urge to open it and read the many note books filled out meticulously by Trone.

Most of Trone's documents are contained in suitcases. For a man who was very rarely in one fixed address for more than a month or two for the majority of his long life, it seemed appropriate that all that can bear testament to him should be in suitcases. Each suitcase tells a story. Sometimes it is a comical story tinged with sad remembrances and subtle truths. Sometimes the suitcase tells you of hopes that end in tragedy, and others tell you of a life lived in great expectation of arriving at some place better. But there was one suitcase that holds the story of thousands, so many voices that the suitcase stands apart, as something beyond the life of one man named Trone.

After several days of chatting with Trone's daughter, about the Russian Revolution and Stalin and the events that had led her father to live in London England, we finally came to the suitcase that had a number of colourful travel markings. Some of the small travel stamps indicated the suitcase had been to such places as Switzerland, France, the Dominican

Republic and the United States. It had held together well over the years, probably because no one had opened it.

We knew what was inside, more or less. Inside would be the documentation regarding the Sosua colonization project, not all of it but the material that related to Europe. The documentation, regarding the events in the Dominican Republic in the late summer and early fall of 1940 was contained in another suitcase we had already seen. That suitcase contained brochures of happy industries Jews farming and having fun in the Dominican Republic, thankful to Dictator Trujillo for giving them land and a safe haven. It looked very good in the brochures, with young happy handsome men and beautiful women in their early twenties sun tanned and healthy. The farming seemed like a mere pleasant diversion from their endless games of volleyball and campfire sing-songs. It all looked too good to be true.

When we opened the other suitcase all that was inside was thick school notebooks. There must have been twenty or thirty notebooks. They were all written in German. Each notebook corresponded to a location. Each location was a concentration camp, where Jews had been rounded up and kept behind barbed wire usually watched over by machine gun nests or sometimes merely by guards with rifles.

This was the history we were seeking staring at us in the face; there was no sugar coating this, no attempt to give a final report or summary. Trone had left the notebooks as they were. This was something odd as it was not his usual method of working. Trone usually disposed of his notebooks once the final report had been given, or at least in many cases he did not take the necessary steps to preserve those rough notes.

Here the notebooks had been kept, and surprisingly a copy of the final report had not been kept. The original report did exist. It had had been faithfully transmitted to the Joint Distribution Committee, those who had requested it from Trone. Usually Trone would take steps to preserve a copy of the final report, this time he did not. The reverse order had occurred.

His final reports and planning proposals were works of art that he would refine almost to a state of perfection. Even in his eighties he continued to seek a greater perfection in his ability to say so much, so eloquently with so few words. This time, the knowledge he had come face to face with was preserved as is, and the final report was a mere note of no importance.

In the notebooks at the top of each page was written the name, sex and age of a person. Then his or her details of life and profession would follow. Usually there was a statement quoted from the conversation made by each person interviewed. Each conversation Trone had was recorded in the same way. Trone would make his remarks on the person and then write either "Ja" or "Nien." If "Ja" they had a chance to live in the sun lit paradise of the Caribbean. If "Nien" they would be denied this and perhaps the only chance of escape from the concentration camp.

There was no mistake in Trone's assessment of the situation. He knew exactly how long a man could work on the little food provided in the camp before he would die of exhaustion. Trone knew how far the fascists were prepared to go in their racial ideology. Before the Final Solution, where the Nazi high command decided to eradicate Jews from Europe, Trone saw clearly where developments were leading. There was only one destination that such an ideology with its industrial network of concentration camps and its economy of slave labour could lead.

Trone had seen the camps, he had talked with the SS officials running the camps, and he saw how the people were used as slave labour. Trone was trained in gathering information and making predictions. He knew, and the people met in the camps knew, and the people who had sent him there knew, that he was to play god. With the lives of thousands he would decide; who would live and who would die was up to him alone.

At the end of his work for the Sosua colonization project Trone closed the suitcase and left it untouched. He and no one else could ever throw the suitcase away, and no one would open it until now. There are times in writing history when you do not want to record anything of what you know, its enough just to let it all go unremembered. Why would anyone want to be a tourist in the valley of the damned? It's all so long ago now, why should we care? Because, it must never happen again and the only way to prevent it happening again is to know that it can happen because it did happen.

That Genocide could have occurred, as we shall see, was because good people did not believe such evil could happen. The impossible was possible. Trone knew that such evil was at work. He saw dozens of concentration camps. He was operating under no illusions as to what was happening. He knew the genocide of the Jews up close, and yet he never lost faith in humanity, he never lost his sense of hope. That is the challenge this history presents to us; to fight for a better world and make damn sure such evil will not occur again.

From our point of view today, we see them all as dead. From the notebooks in the suitcase they are alive and desperately trying to survive and each one of them could have survived. To tell the story of that suitcase you have to know that those represented in the notebooks could have been saved; with so little, with so few, the millions that were fed to the flames could have survived.

Only Hope

Trone had known Joseph Rosen and James Rosenberg for years[1]. Joe Rosen and James Rosenberg were old friends – through change in governments, political persecution and pressures that came from all sides; all three were locked inextricably in a relationship none of them had ever sought, expected or could even explain. Trone must have looked at them both gaunt and staring back at him with eyes that were almost blank with a mixture of shock and determination without hope.

Rosen was a New York businessman that Trone had known since the turn of the century, over thirty years ago. Rosen at one time had business connections in the Russian Empire. Like Trone Rosen had acted as an intermediary with the Soviet Government and the USA. At one time delivering Lenin`s correspondence to Herbert Hoover[2]. Through their mutual interest in Russian and Soviet industry and the frequent times they had found themselves as accidental traveling companions, Trone had developed a deep friendship for Rosen. He had helped Rosen a number of times and in return Rosen had helped Trone.

Rosenberg on the other hand was a corporate lawyer, who was rather adept at handling cases of bankruptcy. Over the course of his life he had gradually become the backbone of the Joint Distribution Committee. This organization combined the resources of a number of different Jewish charities. With their combined resources help for Jews living outside of the United States could be facilitated. Referred to often merely as "The Joint," this organization was the main life line for Jewish Refugees in the Twentieth Century. Over the decades as Trone came to volunteer his help more and more with the Joint, he came more and more to know Rosenberg.

Between Rosen, Rosenberg and Trone, they had masterminded and guided the development of agricultural projects throughout the Soviet Union, resettling Jews for new lives as farmers. Mostly these projects had been successful. Using resources from the Joint, these agricultural projects had been combined with the Soviet Union's desire to establish modern farming techniques. Jewish people who had lost their livelihoods, such as being traveling salesmen, after the change in government were given a chance to start an advanced agricultural colony. New York money from charities, American diplomats and Soviet Commissars had all come together in the hopeful project to bring new life to the impoverished and persecuted community of Jews in the territories of the former Czarist Russia.

Those colonization projects were almost two decades ago however, and today that optimism and spirit of collaboration was just a memory fast fading in the face of a new reality. When Rosen and Rosenberg called upon Trone to go on one more mission for the Joint, Trone knew they were not asking a small thing, they were looking at their last option.

Trone knew that they were either not physically strong enough to go, or feeling not qualified enough to go. Whatever the reason, these were men looking at him as if he was their only hope and that hope was a desperate one. Trone would have to try his best to keep them focused. He would begin at such meetings as he always did with an assessment of the situation.

The Jews had been concentrated in camps in Germany, having no rights, no ability to survive except for the resources such as those sent by the Joint. Over half of the German Jews had got out since the Nazis had taken power. Some who had managed to get out were now in camps across the border in Switzerland, France, Italy and other Western European countries. Since the war had started in September, with France and the British Empire versus Germany, their situation had become increasingly difficult.

The British government was adamant to let as few as possible Jewish refugees into its empire. They especially did not wish them to go to Palestine, which they controlled, for fear it might raise an Arab revolt against them. They also did not want to be seen as favor ing the Jews in any way for propaganda reasons.

The Nazi propaganda at the time said that this was a war they were conducting against the world conspiracy of Jews. This fictitious conspiracy imagined that Jews were trying to kill all the good German people. To counter this charge the British government was distancing itself from anything that could be seen as sympathetic to Jewish people. In this way Nazi propaganda had been successful at isolating the Jews from humanitarian help. Although not known for its anti-Semitism in comparison to the rest of Europe, the British government had done exactly what the Hitler wanted it to do. The British government did practically nothing of consequence while Hitler made the Jews the victims of his systematic persecution[3].

It seemed also that no one was allowing these Jewish refugees to settle in the United States either. The policy of many in the U.S. Congress was to isolate America from the growing conflict. "To keep Europe out of America, and America out of Europe," was the main theme behind the powerful Congressional Dies Committee which sought to prevent radicals from staying in the United States. This committee was looking for a "Fifth column" of agents working for European governments. Jewish refugees were seen as possible enemy aliens working to bring the European war to America.

Surprisingly as Solomon Trone had just discovered the Jewish refugees were particularly feared as being Nazi agents sent by Hitler to commit acts of terrorism. Even though the Joint would select the candidates from the camps and account for them when they got out, they were still under suspicion of being spies and saboteurs straight from Adolf Hitler. Whether through bureaucratic stupidity or disguised anti-Semitism this discriminatory policy had effectively prevented Jewish refugees from getting to America[4].

The Jewish leadership in the United States, whether it was religious, Zionist or otherwise, were relatively silent on the subject of the refugees. They principally did not want to jeopardize the position of President Roosevelt. Roosevelt had tenuous support from the Congress and the Senate; the leadership of the Jewish community did not want to criticize someone they saw as a strong ally. They needed Roosevelt to protect them should something happen. Roosevelt for his part did not see how he could do anything about the refugees unless he could get support from the Congress. The Congress Roosevelt saw as being decidedly against allowing refugees to enter the United States. Roosevelt himself felt that it was dangerous to allow the refugees in, as there were a possible ten million who could qualify as Jewish refugees fleeing Hitler at that time.

In the Congress and at the Senate what Jewish politicians there were had been actively seeking to crush efforts to bring the issue of refugees to the level of political debate. They saw this as something very dangerous, something that if discussed openly could provoke anti-Semitism in America.

Even the Zionists were not particularly helpful. Their main concern was getting weapons, soldiers and infrastructure for building a Jewish state in Palestine. The plight of the European Jews was a secondary issue to the main project, carving out a territory that would be a homeland for Jews. Such a homeland would prevent such a crisis in the future should it ever occur.

All of this was known to the three men. When Trone looked at Rosen and Rosenberg, he knew that they, his two old friends, were the only support he was going to get on this mission. Although the support of the Jewish community outside of its leadership was fully behind the struggle to get the refugees out, their voice was still having no effect upon government policy. The financial support of the Joint was of little concern either as the obstacles were not about money; they were about the numerous bureaucratic road blocks in the way of refugees getting to safe havens. This was the challenge Trone had to overcome; select and guide a lucky few from the slave labour and concentration camps, through the hazards of bureaucracy and eventually to the land of freedom on the agricultural settlement.

It was reasoned by the Joint that the Nazis would let the Jews go, perhaps even, at this time, without a ransom price being paid for them as hostages. The Nazis had not yet begun their "Final Solution." At this time the Nazis were only trying to drive the Jews from their borders by persecution. There was of course almost no where safe for the Jews to go.

The Dictator of the Dominican Republic Trujillo was offering a place for a few Jewish families only, and those were to be of a very particular class and kind. They would largely be farmers and professionals with their families, who were educated in the most sophisticated scientific methods to make an agricultural colony successful. Trone would go to the camps pick out of the refugees that fit the description and then go with them to the Dominican Republic. Trone would see that their new agricultural colony would be set up along the lines specified by the dictator. It would be a modern agricultural colony promoting the most up-to-date ideas about farming.

Trujillo did not want the Jews particularly but he had some crimes he wished to erase from public memory. The dictator was responsible for a massacre of unarmed Haitians when he ordered an unprovoked attack on Haiti a few years earlier. As many as fifteen thousand may have been slaughtered. Trujillo paid some reparations money to the Haitian people but it was not enough to clean up his image as a blood thirsty tyrant. To make himself look better internationally he had publically stated he would take in one hundred thousand Jewish refugees. This would eventually be reduced to around two hundred families, two hundred that Trone would select.

Solomon Trone would have put the situation to Rosen and Rosenberg quite simply. The Jewish community was divided between its leadership and its people, and therefore they were of little help. The government in the U.S. considered the refugees possible Nazis and would try to prevent them from getting to the Dominican Republic, in case they might end up in New York. There was only one place for the Joint to send the Jews and that was a colony in the Bay of Sosua in the Dominican Republic, but only if the refugees were agricultural experts.

To Trone's summary of the situation he would have asked Rosen and Rosenberg if he had missed anything. Their response would have been was an emphatic "yes," he had missed something. What Trone had to be probably told was that he was forbidden from contacting the anti-Nazi resistance. There was little enough chance of success without Trone getting mixed up with the efforts of resistance groups. Trone must have smiled; Rosen and Rosenberg knew him so well. After all these years they knew that Trone was a walking information gathering machine, forever trying to know what was happening, getting to the bottom of every situation. It would be his natural first instinct to find out as much as he could from all the sources he could and that would include the resistance.

Rosen and Rosenberg would no doubt set limits to who Trone could contact, the Passport Office would set limits to where he would go, and events would so overwhelm the situation that both of those limitations would become irrelevant. Trone would set out with a limited set of instructions. When he got there he would find himself in the middle of something much larger than anyone expected. In a world falling apart he would find himself in a situation where many of the threads of his life would come together.

Convergent Destinies

On January 12, 1940, aboard the S. S. *Washington* Trone and his wife Florence set out on their mission to tour as many concentration camps they could[5]. They would interview as many as possible in the camps and write down their identities and life stories. Trone and his wife would not discuss this time in their lives very much.

The 1917 GE-Bolshevik period in Solomon Trone's life would be something he would remain secretive about for obvious reasons. He would always raise a finger to his lips and say nothing if asked. About his 1939 trip to the camps few if ever asked any questions and he and his wife never liked to talk about it[6]. What we know comes from the documentation gathered from firsthand accounts of the work of Solomon and his wife. Of course J. Edgar Hoover's later investigations would uncover many people who were there as well and they had their own very different interpretations of what happened. Some stories did escape the lips of Solomon

Trone, but they did not appear related to the camps unless you knew the context. The context was never fully revealed.

What are we to believe of the different accounts we will explore? Trone did not speak about it; his point of view is not in any real sense recorded. Only in the 1950s in Israel did he give some indication that he had seen in the concentration camps at all. Having had surgery Trone was in a semi-conscious state for days filled with painkillers. In that state he would mumble about the lines, upon lines of concentration camp victims he would see in his mind. They were lining up to ask him for life, life he could not give. Each one he had to let go to their deaths. Once conscious there was nothing he would say about it, and he appeared to the world as little changed by this strange journey that took place from 1939 to 1940.

Florence on the other hand was a different case entirely. Trone knew that Florence smoked occasionally, socially at parties and with friends. Did Trone notice that when she got back from this trip she had taken up chain smoking, and her eyes and hair would never quite look the same again? It is not known, and Trone never said. From photographs we know that when Trone looked at himself in the mirror he would see a man who had aged very little from his 40s to his late 60s in 1939. Even after the trip, Trone looked little changed.

This trip would be one occasion when his ability to focus on a limited set of ideas and gather information around those ideas would be paramount. Trone could focus. It would be a trip that involved extensive driving all across Europe. From landing in Genoa, Italy and setting up a base at the Joint office in Switzerland, Trone would then visit most of Europe. He visited concentration camps in Germany, Italy, France, Belgium, Holland, Latvia, Lithuania, Hungary and Rumania.

Trone began the work on the camps by contacting through the Joint the Nazi government. They immediately sent a car to the Swiss border. The car was driven by a very young SS officer. Trone within a few moments of the drive in German territory had gotten to know the SS officer so well, he had found out that he was unmarried, had a dog he loved very well and had initially joined the Nazi party so he could get more rations, and thereby feed his dog[7].

The SS officer once he had become relaxed with Trone, wanted to give him some gesture to put not him, but his obviously nervous chain smoking wife at ease. The SS officer took off his gun and side holster. He gave it to Florence asking her to hold it for him, as he said it made driving difficult. She accepted and held his gun on all their drives throughout Nazi Germany.

Trone asked the SS officer to pull over at a nearby village. When he did so, Trone walked out and went to a local store and purchased a thick school notebook. On each trip Trone would do the same, purchasing one notebook for each camp. They visited a number of camps in Germany throughout the next months, staying at hotels especially for foreigners. Their driver had to stay elsewhere.

At each camp Trone would be provided a list and would get some idea of who was who in the camp. The commandant of the camp would make an announcement and then the captives would line up to make their case to Trone and be recorded by Florence in the notebooks. In Germany there was not much luck finding his agricultural experts. But Solomon Trone was not just on the lookout for the Joint, he was also gathering lists of names.

At some point Trone had made a trip into Germany without the SS driver. Arriving at a railway at an appointed time he handed half a ripped postcard to a man with the other half of the ripped postcard. At that point Trone had made contact with the German underground. Subsequently each camp then became a chance to be the eyes and ears of the resistance, looking for their comrades, finding out where they were imprisoned, and perhaps finding a way to get them out.

On the way back into Switzerland the Gestapo caught up with Trone and his wife. They searched them completely and then began to interrogate them. Trone of course talked to them without raising suspicions and said nothing to tip them off. Florence had trouble however. The Gestapo captain had found a note from their daughter. Their daughter had written about her birthday party in New York City, where she was staying with her nanny. She had 11 candles, and 5 cherries on her birthday cake, she wished Momma and Poppa could have some of the cake, she missed them so much. The Gestapo captain was sure the candles and the cherries referred to explosive devices that were being smuggled into Germany to sabotage industry. It took sometime but eventually they were released and safely arrived back in Switzerland[8].

From the picturesque safety of Switzerland Trone could contemplate his next move, but he had to be quick. He had seen and knew very well that the German army was ready to invade France. He knew also that the peace between the Soviets and Nazi Germany could not be maintained either. It was clear to Trone that this was a short space of time in which to act.

All manner of people had been rounded up by the Nazis; Jews, ethnic minorities and political opponents were all housed together in the camps. Under the work for the Joint, Solomon had an opportunity to get other people out as well as agricultural experts. He needed allies though to do this, and the Joint was clearly not enough.

His contacts with the Soviets at this point were still at high levels. The Soviet ambassador to America Litvinov had gone to great lengths to keep contact and promote friendly relations with Trone. Knowing that Trone distrusted Stalin, it appears the Soviets had been extra careful when dealing with him. They had given him some time before this point a special position in their hierarchy of people to keep on side. They had told him that if ever he should need anything from them he must write a letter to a certain agency in the Soviet Union, using red ink in capital letters[9]. Whatever he had asked for would be given. Did Trone use this power, at this time? It is not known, but there are a number of sources that claim Trone did make contact with the Soviet Secret Service, the NKVD[10]. Trone was planning something and that would require an extraordinary alliance.

Trone made his way out of Switzerland, this time to make a search in Italy. In Italy he found the situation was truly wretched. The people in the camps had little food and seemed more dead than alive. For their part they had great anger at seeing Trone. In the depths of a crisis, the international Jewish Charities had done nothing to save the people in the camp except send Trone, so it seemed. Trone's sole purpose appeared to be to ask the concentration camp inmates had they ever done any gardening. Trone understood the reason for the anger.

Once Trone had arrived in the camp and gone over the list, he gathered the inmates together and gave them a speech. It was a speech meant to inspire the group. It would be the same speech he would give at all the camps he visited, if he could.

He would say he and his wife were coming to select people for the Joint settlement program in Sosua in the Dominican Republic. Everyone of course would look blankly at Trone; he would know they were thinking "where is the Dominican Republic?" Solomon would speak of the international diplomacy that had gone on to help them, and how this project had come about. He would say that he could get some of them out with visas to go to the Dominican Republic, but only those who were of a certain type[11].

They would need to line up and he would interview them. He needed young pioneers good with tools, at least one in ten must be farmers, and the rest must be butchers, bakers, tailors and mechanics. He would go on to tell the people of the glorious project and how it would be difficult at first, but eventually they would create a wonderfully efficient productive agricultural community using the best that agricultural science could offer. By the end of course no one was really listening, they had heard the word "Visa," and in all the European languages of the inmates, that meant freedom. An entry visa to another country was what each one of them needed to get out of the camp. To be sure they would all line up.

Trone would ask each one in line if they were afraid of hard work. In their diseased, enfeebled, starved state, under the watch of machine gun towers, behind barbed wire, some American was asking them were they afraid of hard work. The question was absurd. For many they had just spent the last few years running and hiding from Nazis trying to sniff them out with dogs and shoot them. Only with the greatest of luck had they got across the border into Italy only to be rounded up in camps to be starved to death. Hard work was the least of their worries.

Each in line was interviewed and their details were recorded by Florence, they would get an answer at once from Trone whether they would be considered or not. The criteria were made clear to the first few in the lineup that were rejected for consideration. Trone was looking for rough looking peasants who could farm it appeared.

The process of selection was clear to Trone as the dividing line between those that would live and those that would die.

> We have seen and lived with the refugees there, and one of the hardest tasks we were up against was to select - we being the judges - who will have homes, who will have sunshine, who will have a chance to live[12].

These first few rejected started to tell the others in the line what they had heard. From that point on each in the line would sound more like a peasant from the village than the last person. By the end of the interviews that went on into the night, an absurd spectacle was taking place.

Each camp inmate would pretend they had lived a life filled with farming, and now they only dreamed of milking cows in some fine tropical country. If only Dr. Trone could see his way to putting their name down on the list for a Dominican Republic Visa, then their dream would come true. They would be forever in Dr. Trone's debt as they would farm till they dropped dead from exhaustion, happy to know that they were creating a scientifically advanced farming colony. Dr. Trone did not appear to mind, although it is doubtful he was taken in by this charade.

Trone of course had no illusions about much of what he saw, in that camp or in any of the camps he visited. He was a trained expert at observation. Although his enthusiasm may have seemed out of place to the camps survivors, Trone stated in his report to the Joint the truth of what he saw.

> This is not enough to cover the most primitive needs...the emigrants are undernourished, poorly clad, and have difficulty keeping clean. The worst is that these people have lost all feeling of responsibility and desire toward any goal. They can do nothing to change their situation. They have become objects of circumstances and powers which they can neither influence nor control. Only very strong people – inwardly strong – can maintain themselves. The majority of them break down ... It is a tragedy, the extent of which can hardly be imagined. Everyone wants to get away – where – it doesn't matter[13].

After seeing a number of these camps outside of Germany, Trone would comment:

> The fear of war here has created a psychosis which particularly depresses the German emigrants; they assume that they will be sent back to Germany, and since they have experienced the concentration camps there, their spiritual condition is a sad one ... It is naturally not simple to find suitable materials for the Dominican settlement under these conditions[14].

Despite this Trone at the time wrote to James Rosenberg that, "We are convinced that we can and will find sufficient good material[15]." In point of fact Trone had more names of suitable people than he could deal with for the Sosua project. Trone would travel to half a dozen countries between January and May collecting names. The names of many he needed to save were not just refugees because they were Jewish some were also political opponents of fascism; some were even his former comrades.

When touring France in particular Trone would run into the exiled opposition to Stalin. These were people under sentence of death should they fall into the hands of either the Nazis or the Soviet Secret Service. As left wing radicals, some who had been deeply involved the political events of 1917, they had been actively seeking the overthrow of both Hitler and Stalin. Their last refuge and exile was Paris.

One such comrade was Willi Munzenberg[16], who as the Soviets Communist International spokesman had fought to create a strong resistance to Hitler in Germany. Unable to keep from being targeted by Stalin, Munzenberg had been ousted from the Communist Party and was considered an enemy of the Soviet Union. For Munzenberg, this was a call to arms. Munzenberg using his skills and resources that he used to fight fascism now fought on a second front internationally against Stalin.

Neither the United States government, nor any other government appeared to want these political outcasts. These comrades of Trone were now looking at the possibility of capture by the Nazis within a space of a few months. They had nowhere to hide and their only chance of escape came in the appearance of their old comrade, Dr. Solomon Trone, GE's revolutionary salesman.

Somehow in Paris Trone had made contact with his old comrades now in exile, perhaps his first contact was with the old Menshevik comrade Feodor Dan[17]. The old comrades sat Trone down and asked him what was going on, and asked him in particular where had he been all these years that they had been fighting against Stalin. According to reports of those at the meetings with the exiles, Trone wept as he talked of what he knew about the Stalinist show trials. He said that Stalin, "Out Czar'd the Czar"[18].

Some at the meeting said they were sure that he was still in very deeply with the Soviet hierarchy; something Trone knew only too well was true. One person would later claim they were convinced when they met Trone again that he must have been the mastermind behind the current peace pact between Hitler and Stalin. Trone had talked about the peace pact as being a necessary evil to give a breathing space to the Soviet Union to arm itself against attack.

Unconvinced of Trone's sincerity many of the old comrades did not believe him either when he said he was in a limited position to help them. They needed out, they were his comrades of old and he therefore had a solemn duty to help them. Trone of course had a limited number of ways to help them. Already the U.S. State Department considered the refugees potential Nazis, each one would be investigated by the FBI. To add these comrades to the list, who were famous and known subversives would be disastrous.

As always Trone did not leave without saying one way or the other if he could help them. This time he could not help, and said so. Some of his comrades who did survive the war would later be interviewed by the FBI. They would blame Trone for almost every kind of diabolical collaboration with Stalin's tyranny. Most of all they would blame Trone for the execution of Munzenberg in France in 1940 by an execution squad sent by Stalin.

The question would hang in the air in the interviews by the FBI; unanswered because it could it never be answered. Did Trone help the NKVD track down Munzenberg in France? In all probability the answer is no. Solomon Trone had a deep hatred of Stalin at this time. He was in no doubt as to the nature of Stalin's tyranny; he had seen it up close from top to bottom. Trone was also genuinely sympathetic to these exiles, but as he said, he was limited. While he may have had contact with the NKVD, their business with Trone was getting their agents out of the SS concentration camps. They would little have wanted at that time to make an enemy out of Trone by asking him to help execute his friends.

This is one time when Trone seemed to hold all the cards and yet in reality could do very little. He still did not have the right connections to people in authority to get the real support he needed to get people out. The colonization project was a joke. At most he could get out two hundred families. Perhaps four hundred people could be saved once everyone had been able to get their relatives still in the camps out to join them in the colony. What Trone needed was someone in a high place in the State Department of the United States. As luck would have it, that is exactly what he was able to find, at just the moment the German Blitzkrieg rolled across the border of France in June 1940.

Caught in the wake of the retreating allied armies fleeing the lightening advance of the Germany military, Trone found himself among the refugees on the roads seeking any place that might be safe. The French government had reconstituted itself in Bordeaux on the west coast of France near the Spanish border.

In all probability Trone had initially gone to Paris specifically to make a plea at the embassy for Visas. Meeting his old comrades had probably delayed him from his task. So if he had gone to the U.S. embassy at this time in Paris it would have been a wasted journey. The U.S. embassy would have already left for Bordeaux. Trone wasted no time and chased them down to Bordeaux.

As the German army had advanced on Paris, the U.S. Embassy had moved to the new location of the French government in Bordeaux. Trone was swimming in a sea of refugees that had piled into the city in hopes that they might be safety from the German advance. Struggling to get through the city, the man in his late sixties was determined that he must get through. Reckless of his safety and his health he needed to get visas for would be immigrants to the United States. The Dominican Republic project was not enough; he needed visas for people to get to New York City where they had relatives and political contacts to continue the fight against Fascism.

When Trone had arrived in Bordeaux he was a desperate man on a wild chase for what was in all probability a lost hope. When Solomon Trone was finally brought in for an interview with the U.S. Consul General, he must have had some surprise. There before him was Consul General Waterman. This was the man who he had met so many years ago in 1916 on the train going to Petrograd[19].

The chances of such a meeting occurring of course are astronomical, but in the life of Trone, the strange becomes the common place and the absurd can often seem quite normal in respect to the circumstances. Trone was constantly in motion forever talking to everyone and so he knew a lot of people all over the planet. It is not so unlikely considering the circles he mixed in that he would eventually meet Waterman again. To make matters even more strange, Consul General Waterman was not really who he appeared to be in one respect. That aspect was his Jewish identity. There is no evidence before this chance meeting that he anywhere on any official documentation referred to himself as Jewish.

As Trone presented the list of names to Waterman that he was trying to get visas for, there must have been a moment of shock and panic. Waterman must have found his Jewish German aunt on the list in one of the camps. Waterman immediately sought a way to get her out. Trone would have had to help him get his aunt free.

Solomon Trone would get many, but not all of the Visas from Waterman that he needed. In a race against time, efforts were made to get Waterman's aunt out of the concentration camp. The camp however was just too wretched and she was just too old to have survived before Waterman could get her out[20]. Already Trone's list was becoming not a list of those who would survive, but those who would die.

In the next few months there was a mad scramble to get visas and transportation. The war and the over-running over Europe by the Nazis had changed many of the carefully laid plans of Trone. He, the Joint workers and Waterman had to find alternatives for the routes out of a Europe almost completely sealed to the outside by the war. The camp survivors would be shipped now via Lisbon, one of the few ports left.

Many of them would get there with the help of Waterman using Visas he had approved.

Trone of course would have to make a trip in advance to Portugal and Spain to make this route possible. On entering Spain he had immediately made contact with the Basque resistance to the Spanish dictator Franco. To them Trone had to decline any joint operations[21]. From FBI reports the contact between Trone and the Soviet Secret Service began in Portugal as soon as came to Lisbon[22], although this could have happened in a number of other locations possibly even starting in Italy.

Waterman's consulship was probably now under suspicion of working with the Soviets and perhaps the Nazis to get radicals into New York City. The State Department had been extremely cautious about allowing in refugees thinking that they constituted possible enemy agents. Clearly something had happened to Waterman that had made him go contrary to the policy. Some would speculate what had gone wrong was his meeting with Trone. After Waterman was reassigned from his Consul in France shortly after this point he would go to Mexico and disappear from the records. After a very brief period of work in Monterrey, there is no evidence of his life after that point, or of his death. Fluent in Spanish, it is possible he merely assumed another name.

Other diplomats at the time gave what they could, contrary to their government policies also, to get the refugees out. Trone would say nothing of who helped him or of how many others had been saved thanks to the alliances he was able to make. What dangers they all had run in mounting this operation cannot be calculated, they all knew the risks were high and they would find no gratitude from anyone. Their help was anonymous for many reasons the survivors would never know. It is enough to do good; it does not require a reason to do good.

Although Trone did not discuss what he had seen in the camps or the efforts he took to get people out, there was some telltale signs of what had happened lost in the paper work in the suitcases. There were little thank you notes, not from the survivors but from relatives who had heard that their loved ones were safe somewhere somehow and all thanks to one man named Trone[23].

Seeds of Turmoil, a Harvest of Desires

In the late summer and fall of 1940, however Trone visited the colony and had a very unsympathetic review of the settlement[24]. What Trone found was that most of the colonists were hoping to get to New York City.

They had lied to him when they said they wanted to build an agricultural colony; successfully lied to him, he claimed. Whether Trone really was fooled or not, he appeared sufficiently surprised to the Joint officials when he came to the Dominican Republic to see the colony.

Upon arrival the people selected by Trone had been inspected by the Joint agents. To a person all of the colonists looked in horribly wasted. Unaware precisely how deadly the camps were, the Joint officials were shocked, beyond belief with what they were seeing. They lost no time in writing complaints to the New York headquarters. Surely Trone had made a mistake picking these people, there had to be better available. Of course what only Trone knew was that these were the best he could find.

The colonists made plans to get their relatives out of the concentration camps, as their first order of business. The second order of business was to get better jobs than farming, preferably something in an air conditioned office that paid well. The Joint officials needed to make this project look like a success. If the word got out that this was a failure then the charity money would dry up in New York City and other projects would be lost.

To placate the angry colonists jobs were created in nice air conditioned offices. The money that was meant to go into the agricultural project was often used to create films and magazines promoting the colony, asking for more donations. The colonists devoted themselves to getting healthy, eating well, getting new clothes and making these advertisements works of high quality asking for more money from their New York City bene-factors.

There were of course some genuine dairy and cattle farmers as well as some butchers who really did want to do some farming. These few then became the models for the farming in the advertisements. While hardly swamped with resources, these industrious Jewish settlers went straight to work organizing a way to get more resources out of what they had. Their efforts were successful in creating wonderful brochures with incredible pictures of sing-songs, volleyball games and of course some farming. Even today these brochures have not lost their appeal. The Zionist Hispanic Caribbean dream mythical though it was, looked wonderful.

The propaganda for the colony was used to raise more money from the charitable minded in New York. The money was desperately needed to buy visas and to provide transportation and whatever other necessaries to get others out of the concentration camps in Germany and elsewhere. That was the priority for the colonists, not milking cows and making cheese. If the mission they had set themselves required duping a few kind but gullible people in the United States, then so be it. The cause was desperate and the colonists had to use every advantage they could.

When Trone saw he may well have considered a scam and he let everyone in the colony know about how below standard it was. He told the colonists squarely that they were making a mockery of the colonization project. Of course Trone must have known that this was the best possible outcome the colonists could achieve. What little they had in this desperate situation they were using to maximum effect to save the others left back in the camps. It is significant that Trone kept his complaints confined to talking with the colonists and to his contacts with the Joint. Trone was happy to let the matter rest once he had officially expressed his surprise and indignation.

In the late fall of 1940 Trone left the Dominican Republic. He now had the project completed as far as was his mandate. He had toured all of Europe and seen the onslaught of the Nazi advance and the slaughter of the concentration camps. He had contacted the resistance forces in numerous countries. It is entirely possible he had made alliances with the NKVD as well.

Being an industrial planning engineer, Trone had also taken note of the industries in the places where he had visited. Many of the camps were used as pools of slave labour for the Nazi war machine. Trone had taken note of this. He had carefully put together a picture in his mind of what places needed to be sabotaged, what places needed to be infiltrated and where the enemies of Fascism and therefore prospective allies could be found.

Trone had witnessed the vast technologically advanced German war machine in all its intricacies and in all its consequences. He knew that this knowledge would be valuable, if not essential to stopping the criminals who were murdering those he had left behind in the camps.

To that aim he had resolved himself to finding work, even at his advanced age of 68. It was at that precise moment President Roosevelt was turning to, an old acquaintance of Trone, William Donovan to build the United States first covert operations agency. The OSS, The Office for Strategic Services, as we shall see was founded it appears by Donovan with the help of Trone. Trone was described by the FBI as "a close associate of William Donovan"[25] and there are reports of an OSS colonel who was a former executive of GE fitting the description of Trone who was training agents[26].

Donovan had been an employee of the US government and had been sent to Russia in 1919[27]. His mission then was to prepare a report on the activities of the political changes in Russia. Now with Trone, he would create a group of agents from the circles of the American radical left and the board rooms of corporate America that would fight to defeat Hitler through covert operations. As we shall see Trone's skills, his knowledge of occupied Europe and his connections to the powerful and the radical in America would prove vital to the development of Donovan's OSS. Trone's politics would not be a bar for Donovan, as he hired many people of communist sympathies. When questioned about hiring communists he answered, "Communists? Of course that's why I hired them."[28] To Trone the fight against Hitler was just beginning.

Endnotes

1   (Federal Bureau of Investigations 1950); (S. Trone, Correspondence from Trone to Swope 1939);
(Ross 1994); (Trone, et al. 2009)
2   (Engerman 1997)
3   (Wasserstein 1979); (Breitman 1985); (Jarvik 1981); (Hamerow 2009); (Zvielli 2009)
4   (Friedman 1973); (Breitman 1985); (Jarvik 1981); (Hamerow 2009); (Zvielli 2009)
5   (The American Jewish Joint Distribution Committee 1939-1941); (Wells 2009)
6   (Trone, et al. 2009)
7   (Trone, et al. 2009)
8   (Trone, et al. 2009)
9   (Trone, et al. 2009)
10   (Federal Bureau of Investigations January 12, 1951); (Hoover, Correspondence J. E. Hoover to State Department and CIA June 13, 1950)
11   (Wells 2009, 110-148)
12   (Wells 2009, 133)
13   (Wells 2009, 130)
14   (Wells 2009, 130)
15   (Wells 2009, 130)
16   (Federal Bureau of Investigations August 25, 1950)
17   (A. Trone 2007)
18   (Federal Bureau of Investigations August 25, 1950); (A. Trone 2007); (Trone, et al. 2009)
19   (Transfers 1939); (Trone, et al. 2009)
20   (Aunt of U. S. Consul Dies In Exiles' Camp 1941)
21   (Trone, et al. 2009)
22   (Hoover, Correspondence J. E. Hoover to State Department and CIA June 13, 1950)
23   (Trone, et al. 2009)
24   (Wells 2009, 189)
25   (Federal Bureau of Investigation 1953)
26   (Smith 1982, 186)
27   (Wagner and Mello 2007, 26)
28   (Brysac 2000)

Chapter 8

INVESTIGATING TRONE, INVESTIGATING THE WORLD

The Life of the Party

On returning to the United States, it must have seemed to Solomon Trone that the entire world of artists, scientists, bankers and politicians had found refuge within walking distance of him. Quite often it appeared they had all taken refuge in his New York City apartment. Party after party of eminent people enjoyed themselves long into the night forgetting their problems in Solomon Trone's apartment. The indefatigable Solomon Trone would entertain them with his jokes and his incredible stories in the numerous languages his guests spoke. As the world collapsed into war and mayhem, the crème of global intellectuals and even some of the most powerful people on the planet were gravitating to the few remaining places that were still safe from war.

Solomon Trone at this time had the opportunity to walk in on Einstein who was working out his physics problems on a black board over at the Institute for Advanced Study at Princeton in New Jersey. Walking in without a formal invite is quite a usual procedure for scientists. Working on a difficult problem scientists often have colloquiums that are conducted at the spur of the moment, with whoever walking in and taking a crack at the problem written on the black board. Solomon Trone, with several advanced degrees and a desire to be sociable with everyone, of course took the opportunity to take the public transit and visit Einstein[1]. It is doubtful of course that Solomon Trone was able to give any helpful advice to Einstein.

The room had several scientists both professional and amateur staring off into space. It was very much like a waiting room full of dishevelled old bachelors, with their hair uncombed and each of them desperately in need of a shave. There were some woman who came in as well, but the day of Solomon Trone's visit there was only three men most of the time. It went up to four men at one point and down to two after he left.

Solomon Trone entered without knocking as the door was open. He was greeted with the complete silence of a semi-lit lecture theatre. Solomon had trouble distinguishing which one was the great genius whose fame now extended into popular culture, Albert Einstein. Once his eyes had adjusted to the room he could see who was who, each being the same type of scientist, each deep in thought, oblivious to everything but the question at hand.

Solomon Trone took a look at the blackboard, saw the problem and then took a seat to think. Before the day was out, someone jumped up and came to the board and made a small mark next to another small mark and then sat back down. That was the total activity for the day. After a few hours Solomon Trone got up and without a sound left. That was his meeting with Albert Einstein. It is not recorded whether they ever exchanged any words at all with each other.

One other German refugee at the time, whom Solomon Trone was to meet, was the playwright Berthold Brecht. Brecht's plays were produced in the Broadway theatre district, and there were many other German refugees in New York as well that were good friends of Brecht's. Solomon Trone's parties often included Brecht. The two would pretend for the delight of everyone gathered there to be Hitler and Stalin, debating each other.

Needless to say the comic effect of Trone pretending to be Stalin and Brecht pretending to be Hitler was quite something. Brecht and Trone could give the mannerisms perfectly of the dictators. With subtle changes each would play with the commonly known sayings and speeches and work it so that the meanings behind the high political speeches came out. The madness of both was ridiculed to the delight of the refugees. Since all the people at the party were either refugees from one or both of the dictators, it was a commonly requested scene that Brecht and Trone were asked to perform. For their part it was something they relished, as their attacks were unrelenting and allowed them to give full vent to the anger both felt intensely.

For the full show, the debate between Hitler and Stalin, the Trones' daughter would be rushed off to bed and two seats were placed in the middle of the room. Brecht would take his seat with arms folded and Trone sat with his fists resting on his knees bent forward. Brecht gave the speech about the pure Aryan blood waving his arms gesticulating like Hitler, while Solomon Trone would answer back with Stalin's speech about the greatness of the proletariat, the masses of the world[2]. As they held forth, it was clear that the blood of the German people was to be sacrificed by Hitler. Trone's Stalin was clear how the masses of the Soviet Union were to be exterminated for the glorification of the great leader. Playing with logical inconsistencies in the ideologies of the dictators' speeches, they made it clear to the audience that there was a psychopathic madness at the center of these tyrants.

Brecht's future quip that if the Communist Party finds the people it rules rebellious then perhaps it should elect new people echoed the criticisms made by Solomon Trone at these gatherings. If Stalin did not want real people, then he would have merely subservient captives to rule, two dimensional characters that say stock phrases given to them by the party, and acting in the way that had been entirely scripted. Solomon Trone's politics was about freedom of thought, independence of action and the education and opportunity for individuals and communities to truly develop their potential.

Also in the audience were philosophers of some note. An important group of German intellectuals surrounding what was known as the Frankfurt School had also relocated itself in New York City. All had been under threat of death and imprisonment by the Nazis. Solomon Trone had good relations with them and knew some of them very well from his days living in Berlin in the 1920s.

One member of the group who Solomon Trone knew personally was Theodore Adorno. Adorno was a social philosopher that had a large impact on the understanding of mass culture in the modern world. He often discussed political issues with Solomon Trone. Adorno's ideas regarding the influence of technology on mass culture may have had some influence from Solomon Trone. It is more probable of course that Solomon Trone was more of the recipient of information rather than the giver of it, in his conversations with Adorno.

Solomon Trone's great gift was for listening and thereby gathering information. At this time, between the winter of 1940 to the summer of 1943, Solomon Trone had many people near him who were considered some of the greatest intellectuals of the age. For a person like Solomon Trone the situation offered a great opportunity, one that he used to full advantage. For three years he met and enjoyed the conversation of economists, scientists, philosophers, political activists, and artists of all types.

Solomon Trone was not the only one traveling and having parties. His old work comrade, Clark Haynes Minor was busy in the late 1930s with anti-fascist social events, for high society. Raising money for refugees from Fascist Europe, Minor was at the forefront of such work trying to show how anti-fascist he really was[3]. For these efforts he would after the war get honours from many governments. Despite these efforts Minor still felt the need to move to Brazil at the end of 1940 along with a number of other GE officials.

It is important to note that Brazil was one of the few countries where no extradition treaty with the United States was in effect before 1964. Although no criminal charges had been laid on these GE personnel, some government investigations could be expected. The United States appeared in 1940 to be ready to go to war with either one or both of the Soviet Union and Nazi Germany which were so connected to GE's profit making strategy over the past three decades.

The employees involved in that business may reasonably have been expected at some point in the case of a war to be investigated as to their connections with these enemy nations. An exit to Brazil certainly did appear a nice and neat way to avoid such investigations; investigations that might bring to light GE's lesser known dealings with the Soviet Union and Nazi Germany.

At this time also the unusual and famous Eisler family trio of Gerhard, Hans and Ruth were in the United States. All three were Communists, all three highly cultured and all three at odds with the world, each other and themselves to one degree or another. Their internal family difficulties, their difficulties with Stalin and their life and death struggle against Hitler are of course the stuff of legend, even musicals and plays have been written about it. Where ever they went of course went the intelligence agencies, documenting everything preserving an incredible record of this family of German Jewish geniuses.

The United States because of these refugees from Germany and elsewhere had become a hothouse of experimentation in science, music, theatre, film, art and politics. Solomon Trone was at the center of it all, enjoying the debates and the discussions, despite the fact that this was merely the peaceful eye of the storm, a brief respite before it too was engulfed in global conflict. Battle lines were being drawn in the United States for a conflict that was to divide the country after the war. Already the forces were marshalling that would create an environment distinctly hostile to such independent and experimental intellectuals who had gathered regularly in Solomon Trone's apartment.

Many who were friends and acquaintances of Solomon Trone would later become informants to the U.S. intelligence agencies. Stalin had also sent agents to New York as well, some of whom were told of an old retired

General Electric Executive who is friendly towards the Soviet Union, and can be depended upon for technical advice. Technical advice here could mean the development of the nuclear bomb, or other military technology.

Somewhere lists were being made of who was a traitor to the United States, who must be interrogated, who must be imprisoned and who must be executed. A division between the righteous patriots and ungodly liberal communists was being drawn in the United States. The list of the ungodly was being drafted once more thanks to the help of J. Edgar Hoover the Head of the FBI.

Solomon Trone of course was once again on the list of those who were of interest to J. Edgar Hoover. Paradoxically this time, Solomon Trone was entirely innocent, which made his situation desperate as it was mostly the innocent who in danger of being caught in the arrests. The guilty, actual spies were aware of the danger and were taking precautions not to get caught. Not only was Solomon Trone innocent, he was also working at this time for the State Department. Unaware or perhaps not caring what was happening Solomon Trone was dedicated to fighting the war effort against the Nazis. In particular he was working with the State Department and through them with the Soviet Union and America's radical left to win the war. Where Solomon Trone and the State Department saw allies, J. Edgar Hoover saw divisions of interest, a cancer at the heart of America to be cut out.

Like all divisions in life Solomon Trone ignored such battle lines and was friendly to everyone. Even if you were Solomon Trone's most deadly enemy, courtesy and friendly conversation was never in short supply. People to whom Solomon Trone had been denounced as a traitor in the Soviet Union or in the United States would be greeted by him with the same good manners as he did everyone.

Pointless acts of anger and insult were foreign to Solomon Trone not because he did not have anger or was without emotion, but that something more important was at stake. It was the greatness of Solomon Trone that he could learn from his enemies just as much as he could learn from his friends. To him it was important to maintain a sense of dignity and decorum always. He felt he was true to the enlightenment idea of being reasonable, rational and keeping a disinterested philosophic disposition at all times.

At times it seemed that Solomon Trone was giving advice at every level and in the most important spheres of government policy. He was seen by the FBI to be meeting regularly with such people as the Labour Secretary Frances Perkins and with the President's closer advisors. Moving between New York City and Washington with great frequency, Solomon

Trone was finding himself in great demand and frequently the lunch guest of the most politically powerful people in America. Always close by were the intelligence agencies watching him order from the menu, chat with his guest and then moving on to the next engagement. All of this was recorded with great detail[4].

By this point in time, Solomon Trone was almost completely under the surveillance of the intelligence services of the United States government. The reason for this round the clock, seven days a week tracking of Solomon Trone was his unfortunate mistake to offer his services to the Land Lease Commission[5].

Designed to give the United States Foreign bases for its military throughout the British Empire in exchange for weapons and items of export vital to keep Britain able to fight Hitler, the Land Lease agreement was central to the U.S. foreign policy at this time. Solomon Trone had applied to join the commission connected with this agreement. Once the application had been made then the security check began into the character and previous history of Solomon Trone.

The first item that came up was Solomon Trone conversation with Marcus Garvey in Jamaica. As we have already seen that particular debate directly led to the denunciation by Garvey's followers to the U.S. ambassador. The denunciation had said that Solomon Trone was working for Stalin. This was an accusation that could not be ignored even if the ambassador at the time thought it was a ludicrous allegation.

Interesting to note, there is a story of one informant to the FBI who stated she was employed as an agent to gather information for the Soviets. She had approached Solomon Trone at a quiet moment after a party. She took him aside and asked him would he like to transmit any information to the Soviet leadership in Moscow. Solomon Trone became indignant with her and stated flatly, "Why should I get you to send a message, that's the kind of thing I could do myself?"

In point of fact it is quite likely that Solomon Trone had more contacts in the Soviet and the U.S. leadership at this time than anyone on the planet. If Solomon Trone had wished to give information to the Soviet leadership, there were numerous ways he could have done so. Also because Trone was well known by the Soviet and the U.S. leadership, a message directly from him would carry authority. Any message transmitted through a third party would have been of lesser importance.

Before long Solomon Trone would claim that he had been interviewed by every security agency employed by the United States government.

Eventually the files on Solomon Trone would become so numerous a filing cabinet in one of the agencies could barely hold all the paper work. That Solomon Trone had to wait so long for the security checks to be completed, gave him time to find alternative employment.

One such alternative to the Land Lease Commission was helping William Donovan. Donovan had been given the directive by President Roosevelt to create a secret service to carry out operations in enemy territory, in preparation for the coming war.

At first Donovan had contacted the British MI5 secret service which had offices in New York City. They recommended to Donovan that he create a similar operation to theirs. He should first hire well educated men that spoke several languages and extremely good at charming people socially. As MI5 was full of aristocrats from Oxford and Cambridge who could do the *London Times* crossword puzzle with a pen in the space of an hour, their recommendation was based on their own criteria. Donovan found this advice hardly appropriate for the work he had in hand.

Donovan needed to work with the Soviets and the numerous resistance groups in Europe that were fighting Fascism. The most effective allies in the war against Fascism were turning out to be Communists. Donovan also needed to be able to mobilize resources and in particular money around the world. These would be used to fund and arm whatever allies the United States could find in its war against the Fascist powers, which by this point included Japan as well as Germany. It seemed to him that he needed to use the resources that were unique to America, its massive global corporations. He would use these big corporations to aid the political radicals he recruited for operations around the world.

Where could Donovan find a man to help him in his quest? He needed someone who was wearing a suit, making big industrial plans in the boardrooms of big American corporations during the day and in the evenings was hatching plots to overthrow global capitalism. Oh where could he find such a strange fish? This man also had to be a big fish in both of those contexts. Where could such an anomaly have been found? The answer of course often was found going to lunch meetings with him on many occasions. That dining guest was not surprisingly Solomon Trone.

How Donovan and Trone met, it is unknown. It could have been during the Russian Revolution, Civil War and Intervention when both were in Russia. It could have been they had never met until the 1940s. There could have been a number of occasions when their paths crossed. Although history does not record when they met, the FBI has a record of the numerous occasions they met and planned the creation of America's first covert action agency.

When Donovan did create his covert action group it was filled with Executives from General Electric and the other corporations some of which affiliated with J. P. Morgan Junior's financial interests. Not surprisingly also its agents were former anarchists and other radicals straight from the Espionage Red Scare list created by J. Edgar Hoover in 1919. Whatever was precisely discussed at the meetings between Donovan and Trone, it is clear they were in agreement about how to fight Fascism. Cooperation with the Soviet Union and the radical left resistance to Hitler was essential.

What Solomon Trone was not so good at was briefing intelligence agents. According to one report, when agents sat down to be briefed by an elderly retired General Electric executive with a foreign accent about where they were to be dropped in occupied France, none of them could understand what was being said. Also it is recorded this instructor, who although unnamed could not have been anyone but Solomon Trone, did not provide enough detailed information to the agents. It was as if the instructor had committed to memory general aspects he had seen regarding the specified targets. Because of this, specific details were lacking when the agents did get to their targets. This caused initial problems for a number of agents.

Solomon Trone was best known for his ability to plan and set up organizations rather than run those operations. It is probably for this reason that Solomon Trone was never a member of the Office of Strategic Services that was eventually run by William Donovan. Solomon Trone was the "ideas guy" of his age. He was also the contact guy who knew just about everyone. Throughout the period of 1940 to 1943, Solomon Trone was forever getting information and dispensing it, to and from, anyone and everyone. This was what Solomon Trone did best, and this situation was when he was utilized to the maximum effect.

Solomon Trone had become part of the intelligence nerve center of Washington and New York City. He had become an appendage to the United States government, a virtual research office and walking repository of valuable information. As the FBI followed him researching who he was and what he did, their conclusion was spectacular. He was with everyone of consequence and he was involved in the most important foreign policy and industrial planning projects of the age.

It was at this moment also that further research was conducted into Solomon Trone's early history. This dug up even more damning intelligence. According to reports from 1917 Solomon Trone was a possible

Bolshevik agent, and an associate of Stalin, Trotsky and Lenin. There seemed to be no end of Solomon Trone's association with political movements throughout the world. If there was a time at which Solomon Trone was not apparently doing something political, the reports had missed it. When all the research was put together the final report seemed too incredible to believe. Either the investigations were wrong or Solomon Trone was the superspy of the age. If they were wrong, why were they wrong? If they were right, how could they have missed such an obvious agent for so long? It's no wonder that when all the investigation details came together the head of the FBI said "this is an amazing story[6]."

There was no end of unanswered questions facing the intelligence agencies as the background check for Solomon Trone to work for the Land Lease Office developed into a full blown investigation into the heart of a mystery. It is perhaps because of this ever widening investigation that Solomon Trone decided to find work outside of the United States. The work he was to find would place him on the other side of the globe, in a place where U.S. intelligence agencies would not be able to track him.

Finding Work in a Chinese Restaurant

In early 1940s a friend of Solomon Trone served Chinese food to the powerful Washington bureaucrats and politicians, and Trone was often a guest at these meals. This man was the great power controlling the finances of the Chinese state, one of the richest men in the world and a graduate from Harvard. He had decided that the best thing that he could do was open up what was in effect a Chinese restaurant. He did not particularly like Chinese food; it is just that people expected it when they were invited over. He would have preferred steak and fries with a bottle of coke, to any of the incredible dishes he served his important guests in Washington. This man was T. V. Soong, one of the most important men in Chinese history in the Twentieth Century.

T. V. Soong was sent to Washington to get support for the Kuomintang party that was ruling China at the time. He needed resources and in particular weapons to defeat both the Communist insurgency and the Japanese invaders who had seized much of China's territory. The civil war had been bloody and the Chinese were facing famines and atrocities that were the worst that the Twentieth Century had seen. T. V. Soong knew that without Washington support, the situation would continue to get worse.

Upon arriving in Washington T. V. Soong had found few allies in the U.S. government. Although technically in support of the Kuomintang, there were far more pressing concerns for them to deal with. The situation in China also did not lend itself to an easy understanding or a clear way to fix its problems even if the situation could be understood. There was a great deal of distrust by the U.S. government of the Kuomintang leadership of Chang Kai-Chek as well.

T. V. Soong realizing he had would have a difficult time getting the U.S. interested in his cause he decided to take an unorthodox method of getting their attention. He started to invite people around to a house he rented in Washington; there he would give them incredible and exotic dinners. The place became so popular with senators, congressmen and bureaucrats that T. V. Soong soon had the attention of the most important people in the United States government. Being such a popular social place also meant that it would eventually be visited by Trone.

To Trone, T. V. Soong was a man with whom he could really have a good conversation. Both were massively educated, both wanted to plan for industrial development and both had time on their hands while they waited for the U.S. Government to make a decision in their favor . Because of Trone's sociability and his incredible knowledge and experience in large scale industrial development T. V. Soong found himself a pleasant companion for discussions. He also found himself a potential employee.

T. V. Soong noted that as an expert foreign advisor Trone might also be useful to the Chinese government. Trone already knew everyone in the leadership of two great world powers, the United States and the Soviet Union. Such a man as this could be useful. Added to this incredible list of contacts, here was a man who had operated in civil wars to build projects of successful industrial development.

From Trone's perspective the advantage of working for Soong was overwhelming. First Soong offered a way out of the United States that paid quite well. Secondly he could do what he loved doing, his work in industrial development. Third he would have a chance to gain insight and experience in the industrial and political world of China, a country that he knew only slightly. As the FBI closed in on Trone, the offer eventually made by the Chinese government would have been too good to resist[7].

At the end of 1943 Trone packed his bags once more and headed to Shanghai. What his position would be is that of advisor to the Bank of China and directly reporting to Wong Wen-How. Wong Wen-How was a Chinese scientist recruited by T. V. Soong to direct industrial development.

Trone was set to work almost immediately finding out as much as he could about China. He was to travel throughout China, where ever he could, see the state of industry and interview whoever he could. With his knowledge he was to help put together a plan for the future development of China.

This is one period of time in which little is known about the life of Trone. We know he arrived in 1943 and left in 1949, and only was outside of China when negotiating with the Soviets on behalf of the U.S. at the end of World War II. In those years in China Trone was interviewed by a number of different reporters and was even interviewed by U.S. Government officials, and yet it is somewhat of a mystery what he did.

In his papers there are references from happy engineers for the great advice given to them by Trone. Sometimes there are references from government officials, one in particular thanking him for using his authority to relieve the hunger of an area that was suffering a famine[8]. Long after Trone had been exiled to London England, U.S. authorities would still be interested to find out what he knew about China[9].

One day near the front lines of the conflict with the Communists Trone was lying in a bed relaxing, and hoping to eventually fall asleep. Trone had been traveling by various means of transportation across China as disguised as to his purposes as was possible. He had been inspecting industrial works first hand without contacting the local authorities. Once Trone had taken his own view of the situation he would then contact the authorities in the area and showing them his commission from the Central Bank of China, he would get a guided tour of the facilities.

Only after Trone had committed to memory the questions he meant to ask and made notes in detail about his observations could he relax and perhaps get some sleep. There was that evening a knock on the door by several heavily armed guards of the Kuomintang. Trone answered the door. The guards barked out an order in order in Chinese and repeated the order in broken English. Trone was to understand that a great foreign dignity was arriving that the local authorities must impress. Unfortunately all their electricity in the hotel had not been working, could he fix it? When he had booked in the hotel he had said he was a traveling engineer.

As it turned out all that was needed was several electrical fuses. It took a little while poking around in the dark, but eventually Trone was able to put the new fuses in and then the lights came back up. With great relief everyone congratulated the kind man for fixing the problem. As they sat around after, waiting for the great dignitary, Trone asked them who they were waiting for. They passed him a piece of paper written in Chinese. Trone by this point had a rudimentary knowledge of the Chinese language and its written characters. Ah yes, said Trone, I know who he is. The soldiers and the hotel owner were interested. "It's me," said Solomon[10].

There is also a curious notation regarding Trone in a book by the respected Sinologist Joseph Needham who worked in China at the same time as Trone. In that notation it states "To Solomon Trone, Electrificatzia, Electrificatzia" – Electrification, electrification. There are few other documents that link the two men together. There was a slight opportunity just before Trone died for the two men to meet, but sadly it was missed much to the regret of both men.

When a temporary truce was held with the Communists, Trone had the opportunity to meet with Chairman Mao Tse-Tung and Chou En-li. The truce had been called so that joint action could be created in stopping the Japanese invasion that had already been underway for a decade. It was not long after the Japanese invasion had been defeated that the civil war began again, with increased ferocity.

As the civil war raged Trone's work for the Central Bank was becoming more and more futile. His work planning for the development of China was to view what existed and then prepare plans for how the situation could be improved by the Kuomintang. In the face of advancing Communist armies from the north, such plans for a Kuomintang China were increasingly senseless. The last place for the Kuomintang to retreat to however, would benefit from Solomon Trone's planning work.

Shortly before the Communist victory in China 1949 Trone had a chance survey the island of Taiwan. On the island Trone was able to find sufficient resources available for the development of an independent economy. The problem was that as a previously held Japanese colony its resource sector and its heavy industries were designed specifically to feed the main Japanese economy. As such Trone was able to make specific recommendations regarding the restructuring of Taiwan and the building of a progressive industrial base that would allow the Kuomintang to have an independent center of operation[11].

Trone did not think that the U.S. ally, the Kuomintang, was capable of developing China. Although Trone said he could never understand fully what the different policy changes of the Chinese government under Mao meant, he was sure that something of Communism's future could be seen in China rather Russia. The U.S. support of the Kuomintang he thought had been a terrible mistake. In a letter to a fellow planner, he stated, "We blundered in China, we are still blundering in Formosa (Taiwan). More blunders will prove too costly[12]."

All the time he was in frequent contact with U.S. and Soviet embassies. Both embassies in China were receiving frequent advice from Trone. From the U.S. embassy the question was asked about the Soviet intentions to China. To Trone, the answer was simple. The Soviet Union was far too devastated to have designs on China. The development of Siberia for the Soviets would have higher priority than the development of China[13].

At this time also, Trone's ally in world development Gerard Swope helped found the Pacific Institute. This institute helped to promote the development of advisors for U.S. policies on China. Whether Trone did give advice to this institute it is not recorded.

India and the Plan

As the situation in China became increasingly difficult for Trone, he started to look around for other work. Knowing that the Kuomintang government would fall any day and that the situation was still too hot for him back in the U.S. Trone badly needed somewhere else to go. Around Christmas time, Trone got a gift that could hardly have suited him better.

The Indian Ambassador to China, Sardar Panikkar, was not into the Christmas spirit as the other Ambassadors were, being a non-Christian. Because of this he liked to invite Trone to his residence with his family so they might enjoy the Christmas period together, doing non-Christmas things. Panikkar and Trone hit it off immediately and not least because they shared distaste for Christmas festivities[14].

Both believed that industrial development on the Soviet model would have benefits for India. The problem was massive poverty and an industry that needed to be re-founded with solid organization and planning. Both problems had been solved they believed by the Soviet development model.

Through Panikkar, Trone landed himself work as advisor to India's first Prime Minister Jawaharlal Nehru. Flying out on the last plane of Americans as China fell to the Communists in 1949, Trone had employment waiting for him in India[15].

The project was supported by Nehru because of his own recognition of comparing the models of Soviet development to possibilities of Indian development. As Nehru had pointed out despite, "defects, mistakes, and ruthlessness, Soviet industrialization is stumbling occasionally but ever marching forward[16]." He had also called the Soviet experiment a "bright and heartening phenomenon in a dark and dismal world[17]."

The employment was to involve extensive traveling throughout Indian Subcontinent just as the partition was being put in place between the newly founded states of India and Pakistan. As Trone traveled around viewing industrial areas across the vast country, he took extensive notes from its industrial engineers, businessmen and local politicians. All their good suggestions he placed down and then submitted to Nehru in the form of a plan that would, if followed, rebuild India.

There were however several problems with the plan, which seemed almost a copy of the one used by the Soviets in 1917. First India had no money to buy the machines from General Electric, and Trone this time did not recommend buying the machines on credit, as the Soviets had done.

Secondly India was a country of many ethnic, linguistic and religious identities. The Soviet model demanded absolute unity throughout the country, the establishment of a central planning structure demanded it. India could never be unified exactly in the same way.

Both of these problems did not seem so insurmountable to Trone. First he imagined that the money could be raised by selling off India's cultural heritage. As Trone stated, "in case a foreign loan does not materialize, India would have to utilize all the inner reserves that she has accumulated over centuries in the form of gold, silver, ornaments, jewels, etc[18]."

Secondly through the belief in and guidance of Nehru, the Prime Minister's office could unite the nation by establishing central organs of government control. Nehru would have mechanisms industrial development directly under his control. Trone pleaded with Nehru to establish such control: "Seldom has a man had the opportunity which history now gives to you: to help the people to create the new social order peacefully. The people are waiting for your call[19]."

To Nehru, Solomon was a trusted advisor who believed in him absolutely. Nehru was however more cautious than Trone. Nehru had an understanding of India that told him that such grand development as here was recommended, would constitute a very serious threat for many of the politically powerful people in India.

Interesting to note is that Trone recognized that India was filled with one advantage that the Soviet Union did not initially have; many dedicated intelligent professionals who were ready to undertake the massive projects. Of course it is these very professionals that had some criticisms of their own regarding Trone. These criticisms can be found in the many interviews conducted by the FBI who were following the movements of Trone at this time.

Criticism of Trone's work, brief though it was, in India fall into three categories. First and perhaps the most important was Trone's distrust of foreign capital. Secondly was Trone's use of other peoples' ideas and third was Trone's dangerous tendency inherent in his suggestion of increasing the power of the Prime Minister[20].

No one understood precisely why Trone did not want India to take out massive loans from the West. It was not just on theoretical reasons, as a Marxist that Trone did not want to deal with the Capitalists, there seemed to be something more to it.

In a letter to a friend Trone states, "There was a ten day Indo-American Conference in Delhi. America was well represented. Here you could see the clash of interests. Here you could see East and West Striking each other[21]." To Trone the big business interests of the U.S. were barracudas hungry to gobble up India. Although he did not advise attaching itself solely to the Soviets, he was very wary of the conditions attached to foreign loans.

No one of course knew what had exactly been Solomon Trone's full experience with the Soviet Union. He had of course told anyone who wanted to know about his work in the 1917 October Revolution. He did not hide he was close to the Bolsheviks and that he saw "all the phases of the revolution." Solomon did not mention about the role of General Electric in the planning of the Soviet Union, nor of any help provided by any of the corporations associated with J. P. Morgan Junior. Of this Solomon was silent, making his fear of the West's capital even more mysterious.

The second problem with Solomon Trone in India is probably the most interesting. Solomon Trone was not paid for being an industrial planning expert but he did ask for his expenses to be paid, which included a plane trip to Brazil to visit his son. These costs for a poor country such as India seemed rather large and excessive to many. Especially so, it seemed, because on closer inspection all of the proposals of Solomon Trone had been taken from speaking with Indian professionals.

This of course is what Solomon Trone did, he found out as much as he could from the experts present and then put together a report combining and harmonizing all those opinions. Trone was in essence a conduit and a catalyst for bringing together ideas that already existed. Solomon Trone never claimed to be doing anything else. Still, it was mused, could not an Indian have been found who could more easily combine the ideas of other Indians?

The third and perhaps the most damning reason was that Solomon Trone was favor ing more centralized power in the hands of the Prime

Minister. This was the reason Solomon Trone left India. It appeared for many that their power as local and regional leaders was directly threatened by Solomon Trone's one India industrial policy. If you build a centralized industrial planning structure, you enhance the central government's power to dictate its control of the entire economy. Minority interests are an essential reality of Indian political life; any centralized system would necessarily run the risk of over-ruling those interests.

Solomon made a number of close friends at this time including the great planning expert Gyan Chand, who his family lived with. While he did not lack support, particularly from Nehru, there were significant opposing factions that represented a decentralizing force in the Indian nation. The centralizing tendencies of Trone's planning suggestions could not be established in such an environment. Solomon Trone, against the wishes of Nehru, decided after one year that he should leave India. He had given his recommendations, but the Indian government was not yet ready to institute his ideas.

At the end of Trone's stay in India he and his family were invited to live with Nehru for two weeks. In those two weeks Trone and Nehru went through a step by step breakdown of where Trone had been, who he had talked to and what of importance he had discovered. After a year of extensive traveling, countless interviews and in depth hands on investigations into the industrial infrastructure of India, Trone had prepared for Nehru a broad report on what industrial development could be done and how that development could fit within a plan[22]. It took two weeks to of intensive review for Trone to fully relate what was in the report.

Trone's report may have been complex and detailed, but his argument about India's development was not. What India lacked is not money but the correct perspective and the national spirit of forming a united front. India is the only exception among the big countries in industrial progress. Indian methods and means are antiquated and inadequate to cope up with her requirements. India has vast resources and a big consuming market. These can be utilized for developing the countries industries.

In the end Trone and Nehru would be sitting side by side at an impasse. Nehru understood exactly what Trone was saying, but he disagreed. He did not disagree in principle; theoretically what Trone was saying was possible. But to do what Trone was advising would have the effect his critics were warning him about. This approach would tear India apart by centralizing and making India one planned and standardized political economic system. In a speech Nehru had said, "I do not rule out anything, but I do rule out being uprooted from India, may be, made into some kind of hot-house plant which may look in the hot-house beautiful but has not roots anywhere in this country."

To Nehru the plans suggested by Trone were in many ways, a prudent way forward, in others they would break irreparably the life of the village in India. Something would be lost of India's identity. Trone argued against this point of view, but he and Nehru could not finally agree. The reason why Trone left India is simply that his planning advice although respected by Nehru could not be practically implemented.

The Unplanned Promised Land

The least effective planning work Trone ever did was in Israel. Some recently in print have lamented that Trone's advice sensible and practical in every way was never listened to. At the time his advice although initially requested by the government was flatly ignored. He never had a more thankless job than when he worked for the Israeli government. His notebooks surveying the country are both extensive and detailed[23].

Trone was not a Zionist. His brothers were and they were very dedicated Zionists as well. Trone's brothers had risked arrest in the time of the Czar organizing Jews throughout the Russian empire to found a new country in Palestine. Trone did not get on well with his brothers and sisters, especially on political matters. The defining difference in the family was the support or opposition to Zionism[24]. Trone was defined first and foremost as a Non-Zionist. Of course, as we have seen, Trone would spend most of his adult life dealing with one Jewish colonization project or another. Why should the Jewish colonization project of Palestine be any different to those projects?

Trone said he did not know exactly what "Zionism" meant, as it was a concept full of contradictions. It was a return to a land that had been left thousands of years ago according to a book supposedly divine that he could not believe. To reject the Jewish religion that forbade a return to the land before the coming of the Messiah and yet because of that Jewish identity return to the land, seemed at least a little confusing if not contradictory. Trone would have no dealings with the idea of Zionism, but on a practical basis he was more than willing to help build Israel.

Staying at the King David Hotel, Trone arrived in the newly formed state of Israel on January 1st 1950. He would spend the next six months reviewing the present industrial structures of Israel and interview hundreds of people in positions of authority. After his review he would then spend several months putting together a report detailing a plan for the industrial development of Israel. Trone's final report would not be presented until June 1952.

The report would have been created sooner, but there were several problems that Trone faced at this time which delayed the report. The first problem was his hip. He required surgery at this time due to problems with his hip, presumably a fracture sustained while traveling extensively and continuously since leaving New York City in 1943. It was also not an easy recovery for Trone, and he spent many months unable or at least limited in his ability to walk.

During this time Trone had time to discuss the development of the report with the Israeli government. They did not like his recommendations and they had made it clear, the recommendations would not be followed. They wanted something very different from the plan Trone was offering.

Trone's plan was based on the German war reparations that were to be paid to the Israeli government. The post-war German government had decided to pay an indemnity to the Israeli state, in some measure to atone for the genocide of European Jews during World War II. This indemnity would be paid mostly in the transfer of industrial technology to Israel. Trone was to come up with a plan for this transfer of industrial capital.

Trone had seen firsthand almost all of the large industrial structures in Israel. After China, Russia and India, the review of this "microscopic" country for Trone seemed a simple matter. While the review of what existed was not difficult, coming up with a plan presented great difficulties. To Trone the most important element was to build the industrial infrastructure first and then allow industrial corporations, private or public to develop within that industrial framework[25].

The Israeli Government had other ideas. They wanted the transfer of industrial capital straight to the industrial corporations that would then develop. These corporations could be public, private or cooperative. Where as in Trone's model, it was infrastructure first and then the development of the corporations, in the government's model, the model that would be implemented, the corporations developed first and then the infrastructure followed.

For months Trone tried in vain to convince the government of his proposals. The government, on the other hand, wanted a plan that fit their proposals. Between the two there could be no agreement. Just like in India and China, Trone had researched in depth the industrial infrastructure and completed the planning for industrial development in a report that would be shelved and never implemented. His plans were to become the basis for understanding what the country he was investigating was like at the time and give an alternative future to the one that did develop. He developed a picture of what was and what could have been.

For Israel, there would be no discernable direction behind what type of a country they wanted. For Trone, this was an anathema for the way he worked. There had to be a vision for the society you wanted to create. From point "A" where you were at that moment you had to have a point "B" where you wanted to go. Trone could tell you exactly what the industrial state of affairs existed at point "A" and could tell you exactly how to get from there to where you wanted to go at point "B." Without an exact destination however, Trone's ability to chart a course into the future was useless. There was no where to go, there was no vision for the future.

The grand technocratic designs for the development of societies often overnight on the scale of a continent required one thing more than anything else; it needed a singular ideal of the society you wished to develop. The Israeli people simply could not decide on what they wanted for the country. To this day Israel lacks a constitution, the one element that could define it as a nation. Out of many different countries, with many different traditions and many different ideals the Israelis had formed themselves into a nation, but they could not agree on what was the exact nature of the society they wanted.

The failure to define exactly what they wanted their society to develop into, meant that it could not set goals for the infrastructure that would define how future development would occur. To Trone this was a failure once more to have a unitary idea of what the development goals would be.

In China Trone had seen that the civil war meant planning was not possible. There was no single country to develop but two fighting for control in one territory. As such no development planning was possible. Trone's experience in India showed that where there were many areas that were essentially distinct, centralized and all-encompassing development goals could not be established. Here in Israel a similar limitation had been reached. Where there was no firm consensus about what should be developed, as in Israel, Trone saw that industrial planning on a grand scale was almost pointless.

The ideal of the centralized industrialized state built with massive corporations on the model of the United States, once admired by everyone, now seemed to be a good deal less desirable. What Trone was selling, no one appeared to want anymore. The era of grand industrial designs was over, and a new idea of a decentralized and flexible development was starting to emerge. Trone was to lament this new reality in his final plan to the Israeli government: "The word 'planning' is often misused. In the minds of many 'planning' is an annex: to a totalitarian regime[26]."

In 1953 Trone had become convinced that his plans for Israel would not be implemented, and he was ready to move on to another project. Unable to move back to the United States due to an increasingly hostile political climate, Trone decided to find a place to live in England where his daughter was enrolled in university. It was a move that would create a final exile for Trone, and effectively end his work for radical political ideals.

Endnotes

1   (Trone, et al. 2009)

2   (Trone, et al. 2009)

3   (Minor Dies 1967)

4   (Federal Bureau of Investigation 1945); (Federal Bureau of Investigation 1949); (Van Kleeck 1935- 1943); (Federal Bureau of Investigation 1953)

5   (S. Trone, FBI application - Lend Lease 1943)

6   (Federal Bureau of Investigation 1945)

7   (China Defense Supply 1943-1945); (S. Trone, Correspondence to Yin, (November 12, 1945) 1945); (S. Trone, Biographical statement regarding passport 1953)

8   (S. Trone, Letter Regarding Famine Relief, China 1948)

9   (Hoover, FBI J. E. Hoover Regarding Trone 1958)

10   (Trone, et al. 2009)

11   (S. Trone, General Report on Taiwan, unpublished manuscript submitted to the National Resources Commission 21 January 1948); (Wang July, 2002)

12   (Trone, et al. 2009); (S. Trone, Correspondence from Trone to Carwell 1950)

13   (Meeting Senator Marshall and S. A. Trone 1948)

14   (Trone, et al. 2009)

15   (Mr. Trone Arriving in August 1949) (Aunt of U. S. Consul Dies In Exiles' Camp 1941)

16   (Nehru, Introduction to M. R. Masani, Soviet Sidelights (1936), rpt. 1972)

17   (Nehru, Toward Freedom: The Autobiography of J. Nehru 1941)

18   (S. Trone, Confidential correspondence Trone to Nehru 1949)

19   (S. Trone, Confidential correspondence Trone to Nehru 1949)

20   (Nair 1950)

21   (S. Trone, Correspondence from Trone to Carwell 1950)

22   (S. Trone, Brief Outline of my Engineering Experience 1949)

23   (S. Trone, Israeli Survey Workbook for Development Programme Report 1951)

24   (Trone, et al. 2009)

25   (Rabushka Winter 2001)

26   (S. Trone, German Payments: Basic Development Programme (for Israel) 1952); (Trone, et al. 2009)

Chapter 9

END GAME

Another Future

In New York City on a day in the middle of May 1945, Trone was happily enjoying a moment of peace in his busy life by walking down Broadway in Manhattan. At the age of 73 he was very active, loved to walk, and on this particular day he felt at least twenty years younger. In the shadow of the sky scrapers Trone felt at home again, for the first time in years. We know something about that particular day because it was recorded by an informer and decades later his recollection was published[1].

Trone or Papa, as he was commonly known at the time, had a diplomatic passport as an employee of the State Department. His presence in New York City without the protection of his diplomatic status would have meant an immediate interview with one secret security service or another. Now however he was free to enjoy what was a lovely spring day in a city he loved.

He had just given his report to the State Department. He had also right after that given his much more important report to the corporate lawyers on Wall Street. Those lawyers represented some big interests that had been very worried about Trone's meeting with Stalin's negotiators. He was free to enjoy all the sights and sounds of New York City, the one place he could truly call home.

The air was fresh and the streets were full of busy people going about their business. The world of May 1945 in New York City was one of peace and getting on with business. Although still at war with Japan, there was a great sense of relief in the air that the Germans had surrendered.

Trone had just come from the depths of Civil War China via the bombed out remains of Berlin, on business for the Department of State. He missed this place sorely. He had memories of New York City going back fifty years. Some of those memories were of escapes and secret meetings. On a number of occasions he had been a wanted man in New York

City by the FBI. He had always evaded their grasp though, and now he was fairly sure he could still keep ahead of the game.

With Trone that day walking down the street was a police spy. Although suspicious of him Trone had actually invited him to come along. The man was an old friend of Trone, and he had also known his father in rather unusual circumstances back in 1917. Their chance meeting that day made Trone very happy as he wanted to talk with someone as he went about his day's business.

The police spy, Nathanial, was mentally taking note regarding everything Trone did, but not necessarily everything he said. Nathanial thought Solomon was an incessant and brilliant talker. Nathanial felt he could not give even close to an account of Trone's voluminous conversations. He had once said that Trone could "buttonhole a farmer's son to discuss the existence of God and spend four hours doing so[2]."

It does not appear that Trone cared whether Nathanial was a spy or not; he had already had serious differences politically with Nathaniel. Solomon was well aware that the intelligence agencies in the U.S. were keeping close tabs on him. No doubt Nathanial would be contacted at some point for information. To Trone it was very likely that all his friends and associates would be interviewed by the intelligence agencies about his activities at one point or another.

Open and honest about his opinions, Trone was prepared to face trial and possible execution. He neither feared such a destiny nor tried to avoid it. Now in his in his seventies, he was more than ready to make such a sacrifice. As it would eventually turn out, he would live only three years shy of a century and never face trial. While his friends the Rosenburgs would face trial and execution by electric chair, Trone would end his days in relative luxury.

The fashionable and happy environment of New York had not been hit by the bombings of Europe or seemingly had it been affected by any of the deprivations of war. Trone had just gone and got himself a new suit from his usual tailor. Having just signed a deal that would help give the world peace and rebuild a war ravaged Soviet Union Trone was satisfied. There was hope again in the world. In Moscow, they were singing his praises in the halls of the Kremlin. One of the Soviet delegation members negotiating with the Americans had described Trone as a "dear friend, who loves Russia[3]."

Added to his satisfaction was the mail he had just received from many grateful people. They had learned their relatives had been saved from death in the concentration camps by Trone. The mail for Trone had been accumulating with his lawyer at 120 Broadway. Visiting the law office where his mail had been accumulating also gave him the chance to settle a few other administrative necessities as well.

On that lovely spring afternoon in May Trone had just come from visiting Dick Scandrett, in his lovely house on Pine Avenue. The two had been working together in Moscow just recently. Scandrett was a lawyer associated with the financial interests of J. P. Morgan Jr. and was also one of the leaders within the Republican Party. He was an old and very close friend of Trone.

In Moscow Trone had made Scandrett do all his shopping for him and had him run numerous errands as if he was his secretary. Partly this was Trone's sense of humour, getting such a powerful man to do such menial tasks, but mostly it was important for Scandrett to get a working knowledge of the Russian language. It was equally important for Scandrett to get to know ordinary Soviet people that he was assigned to help through United Nations Humanitarian Relief Agency.

Scandrett had been chosen to lead the United Nations mission to help rebuild the most devastated areas of the Soviet Union, after the Second World War. Trone wanted Dick Scandrett to not be some faceless UN bureaucrat dispensing funds to an equally faceless Soviet bureaucrat. Trone wanted his good friend Dick to get out of his office and his chauffeured car and be a hands-on director in rebuilding the areas destroyed by the Nazi war machine. When Dick had finished his job for the UN he acknowledged that Trone's method of getting down and dirty was the correct one. Dick's mission would be a success thanks to Trone's pushing him to know Russian fluently and understand the Soviet people better.

On that May afternoon in 1945 a very satisfied Trone walked down the New York City sidewalk at a brisk pace, even though he was in his seventies, it was as if he were a much younger man without a care in the world. Going from office tower to office tower in Manhattan, doing all the business that had been mounting up for him to do in the several years while he had been away, Trone was looked neither tired nor bored. Trone seemed to grow in strength at every meeting. It was as if each person he visited said the same thing, "My god, you are still alive! Papa, tell me where have you been all these years?"

At this point in Trone's life he had survived the most dangerous events the Twentieth century had to offer. He had come face to face with civil wars, revolution, Stalin's purges, Hitler's concentration camps and he had been investigated at this point for thirty years by J. Edgar Hoover. Having survived it all he somehow knew that even if his travelling companion was a police spy, it did not matter at all. Everything about Trone was an open book.

We know about this day in Trone's life because of the police spy, to whom we should be somewhat grateful. It was the police spy's lucky day for having things to record. First it was lucky because he had met up with Trone at all. Trone was not in the country for very long before he had to leave for a number of reasons. The second reason Nathanial the spy was lucky was because the person Trone was going to visit was also under suspicion by the security agencies. To give information on two suspects of high treason in one report made him a very important informant.

The person Trone was visiting was Ruth Fischer. She was in her later years now and she was the former head of the German Communist Party. A onetime dissident to the rule of Stalin, Ruth was now advocating a renewed invigorated worldwide Communist movement.

Trone was expected. He walked out of the elevator at the right floor and straight to her door. They waited a moment and then they were greeted by a lady in her late fifties, with a heavy German accent. Trone introduced Nathanial to Ruth. Ruth invited them both in.

She asked them to join her in her study. Her study was a sunlight room that had a big desk and the walls could not be seen for book shelves that went from the floor to the ceiling. Many of the shelves were filled with loose notes bound together with pieces of string. There were reports and books in several languages as well, including some that looked like books about art.

Ruth was from a very artistic family and her brothers had written a number of orchestral scores for movies and the theatre, as well as political songs that were famous the world over.

Laid out on Ruth's desk were a number of newspaper clippings from what appeared to be Spanish language newspapers. Next to a paper try was a small weighing scale. No doubt the scale was used frequently as Ruth was often corresponding with people and sending copies of her writings for publication. She probably needed to weigh each package and letter to figure out how much postage to pay. Like Trone, Ruth had become very efficient at keeping her administration.

When Trone was in the room Ruth asked her guests to sit down on the couch near the window. Ruth pulled a chair around to face Trone, but she did not sit down. She asked them if they would like a drink, perhaps tea. Both guests declined the offer and Ruth sat down.

She looked at Trone and asked him directly, "What have you been doing?"

This was always a dangerous question with Trone. The risk was that he just might tell you. This time, he did not say much, just that he had been busy in China, acting as an adviser to the Central Bank there. What he had

161

really been doing there and what he had been doing so recently in Berlin and Moscow was something he did not discuss. It would, however, have been of much greater interest to the former head of the German Communist Party, Ruth Fischer, than his work in China.

Trone saw Ruth nodding her head; perhaps she knew that more could not be said. Trone then asked her, what she had been doing of late. Trone had already noticed numerous documents on her desk in Spanish. Ruth looked directly at Trone with a sudden intensity that made Nathanial nervous. Trone was not nervous however, he was curious. It was normal for Ruth to be passionate about her work.

Trone learned that Ruth had been to Latin America and had investigated the working conditions and the level and type of political awareness there. It was promising. As one revolutionary to another this was something to take note of. In these countries, especially Cuba, they were dispossessed of land and had leaders that were little more than dictators appointed by Washington. More to the point though, the people there had advanced political ideas that were unique and did not follow the party line from Moscow.

Trone only a decade before had been in the Spanish speaking areas of the Caribbean also, he knew what she was saying. Trone had done similar investigations. He had talked with whoever he could, taking note of the industrial structures as well; who owned what and how much was controlled by Wall Street.

Ruth and Trone discussed and compared their observations for several minutes. Trone had assured Ruth of the accuracy of her observations. Trone was perhaps one of the foremost industrial planners of his age and his experience by that point was unmatched by anyone on the planet. If Trone said such an observation about the economic and industrial structure of a country was correct, then it was beyond debate. Trone could see that now Ruth was ready to deliver her predictions based on the observations that they were in agreement with.

There would be a workers' upheaval in the Caribbean, most probably Cuba. They would destroy the puppet governments. These changes would not fit the ideas of what people expect of a revolution. They would end up destroying both American Capitalist and Soviet Socialist ideals of how to run both an economy and politics. It would not be business as usual anymore, when it would succeed.

It would spill over into Latin America and a new political force would be born. Out of the collapse of American-Soviet control, there would be a truly internationalist overthrow that would liberate in ways the Soviet Union never could. There were too many elements favor able to its development for it not to occur. It could be delayed, perhaps by decades, but something significant would develop.

Trone looked over to Nathanial who seemed very worried at this speech. It was dangerous to speak of a activities to overthrow U.S. interests in Latin America. Perhaps Nathanial thought he could get implicated in this conspiracy, just by hearing it. Nathanial indicated to Trone that they should go. Trone complied, thanking Ruth for her kindness in meeting with them. He shook her hand, and said how pleasant it was to see her again, agreeing with everything she had said.

Outside of the apartment as they started down the street Trone was finding tears welling up in his eyes. Nathanial looked at him with some surprise. As if by way of excuse Trone looked at Nathanial and said rhetorically, "Isn't she a wonderfully brilliant woman?"

Trone had worked all his life to establish what was now apparent to everyone as the Second World War was coming to an end. There were now two great powers, and two great economic political systems, both of which owed their current form and global dominance in large measure to Trone. Now Trone looked to a world in which both of those systems would collapse and something better would take their place. At the age of 73 he saw a better world emerging from the present global society, he longed to see that change take place.

The great conspirator, the radical from Wall Street and the man who sold the plan for the development of the Soviet Union to the Kremlin, was now contemplating the overthrow of a world order he had helped put in place. Barely was the ink dry on the peace deal establishing the two global superpowers of the Soviet Union and the United States.

Trone did not owe allegiance to a country or an ideology; he loved a future world, a world not yet born. The future was the commodity he traded in, it was the homeland he never was quite able to get to. When he sold the idea of political change to Wall Street, or a grand economic development scheme to Lenin, he was selling a version of the future that was nothing more than an idea of what could be.

To Trone there must always be something better. To many it seemed the future did not exist until he sold it to them as a complete package of plans diagrams and projections about how everything would be better. Out of nothing Trone had created a new and better way in which the world would operate. To Trone however, it was never good enough.

To the police spy Nathanial, it was clear from this that Trone was a dangerous man. From his report and many others taken at that time and after, it was clear to the FBI that Trone was a dangerous political subversive, perhaps a lone independent operator who was as much a danger in his old age as he was when he was younger.

Trone would shortly have to leave to go back to China. His diplomatic mission over, there would be no protection from the investigations of the security apparatus in the United States. As the reports mounted up in the years to come, it would take until 1953 until the intelligence agencies would make a final decision on the arrest of Trone for treason and espionage.

Time to Forget

It is quite unclear why Trone was not taken into custody when he went to the US embassy in Israel in 1953. From what can be found and from interviews what is clear is that he Trone was known as a person of interest and the file on him was now phenomenally large.

We can imagine the U.S. intelligence agent having a somewhat stunned expressed as he looked across the ill lit room in the Tel Aviv embassy on a day in early January in 1953. Here across the desk was either one of the bravest, honest and most unusual men he had ever met or something was seriously wrong with the world. In either case the intelligence agent had two choices, one arrest him immediately and let the pieces fall where they may or let him go. The choice was a strange one because Dr. Trone was eighty one and despite this he was perhaps, according to his intelligence file, the most dangerous man on earth.

The intelligence agent had discretion whether to arrest Trone or not. For some reason Washington did not appear too eager for this man's arrest and this made the intelligence agent uneasy. Something was very wrong with this situation. Here was a man who should be arrested and yet this same man had taken no steps to avoid arrest. The U.S. government was not pressing for his arrest either. Trone had simply walked into the embassy ready to talk about anything and everything. By sheer chance the intelligence agent investigating him was there to meet him. Technically he could have the man arrested or at the very least start the process in motion.

He had just asked Trone what he thought of Soviet style planning. It had some good features he said, and he should know he had helped design them. The intelligence agent had asked him what he thought of free market competition and the values of capitalist individualism. Trone said it should be suppressed and industries should be organized to work in harmony. "Why did he say that?" the agent questioned. Trone then said he was a committed revolutionary throughout his life, and did not see any reason to stop now. The man was talking himself into a conviction for high treason and did not appear to be at all worried. It was as if he were inviting arrest.

I find it impossible to believe he is a Soviet spy, thought the agent. He gave Trone a puzzled look. "If you had talked like this before the House Committee on Un-American Activities you would soon find yourself on the electric chair, being executed."

"I would love to appear before that committee, I would tell them everything, especially if it led to my execution. I am ready to tell all."

The agent sat back. Here was the essence of his dilemma. He had just read through six feet of files on Trone. Trone had been implicated in handing the atomic bomb to the Soviets. Trone had also been an advisor to the President of the United States. While facing a possible charge of treason he did not care whether he lived or died and desired nothing more than to tell everything he knew to the world. There was no dissembling here, no evasion, nothing hidden.

Trone was perhaps an agent of the Soviets working directly for Stalin, definitely an agent of the State Department working directly for the President, a trusted one time employee and friend of very rich people back in New York, a probable follower of Trotsky, a revolutionary double and triple agent that worked for all sides at the same time. No, the intelligence agent could not make up his mind what to do. Nothing here was clear; nothing made any sense to his way of thinking.

If Trone should speak out in public and this version of history known, the intelligence agent could not calculate the ramifications. It was way beyond him. According to Trone's file, the American government and its richest people had aided the Bolsheviks from the very beginning at the very heart of the Revolution. Trone also knew of deep connections between the United States and Hitler's Fascist government. Now here was this enigmatic man telling him that Israel was not what it appeared to be either.

Nothing he knew was true in world politics and history, everything in the world including the current Cold War was apparently due to plans created at high levels by bureaucrats and technical experts such as Trone. The difference between high level long term technical planning and obscure conspiracies seemed to blur for the intelligence agent the more he thought about it.

On the one hand Trone's life pointed to the world mostly being run by high level intrigues hatched by the unholy union of Bankers and Bolsheviks. On the other hand it also suggested that the world's leaders were far more inclined to negotiate with each other and come to some kind of arrangement rather than to risk conflict. Both versions of history were in Trone's intelligence file, and both versions could not be true.

The world is divided between good and bad; you are either on one side or the other. The idea that the current Cold War was in reality a peace between two cooperative powers that had in agreement divided up the world between them, seemed not only to defy conventional wisdom, it seemed subversive in the extreme. In Trone's world there was no division of ideologies, there was a synthesis of complementary ideologies between two powers dependent upon each other.

The intelligence agent tapped his fingers on the desk. What was he to do? Some parts of history are better left buried, he thought. Trone's testimony would damage the anti-communist cause, more than help it. The testimony would raise questions as to the differences between the two sides in the Cold War. An America run by massive corporate structures and a USSR run by massive corporate structures, according to Trone were created pretty much out of the same designs, by the same people, around the same time. As preposterous as it sounded, some people just might believe it, even the intelligence agent was coming close to believing it. This created doubts, a dangerous weakness when facing the enemy.

He decided to ask one more time just to make sure. "Would you tell everything?" asked the agent.

"Everything," said Trone with a satisfied grin.

The intelligence agent looked down at the floor and shook his head. This was one story that must never get out, a history that must never be told. It would be best if the truth were buried with Trone when he died, and considering the age of Trone, that day did not seem too far away. The strange incredible history of Trone, it had been decided by this particular intelligence officer, must not come to light. It was way too hot for him to handle.

From what little evidence of the meeting we have this would appear most likely as to what happened. Although it is possible a decision had already been taken and this was neither the right moment nor the right place for the US government to act.

Not surprisingly Trone would have his passport taken away within the year, leaving him stranded as a person of no nationality in London England, unable to speak before the Congressional committee, or be arrested and put on trial. The reason for this exile however was not because of any decision by the intelligence services, at least as far as we can discern from the documentation available.

The reason of Trone's exile was not to bury or silence him as might be imagined. Still ten years into the future, the intelligence agencies would be indecisive about Trone, still wanting to gather more information about him, still wanting to interview him and perhaps put him on trial. The secret service men were always too confused about Trone to act.

One person however was not too confused to act. Although she was not in the secret service she would act and act decisively to exile Trone to home in England for the rest of his life. That person was the head of the passport office, Ruth Bielaski Shipley.

Passport to Retirement

By 1953 Ruth Bielaski Shipley was hailed as the great guardian of America, the patriot that stood between it and the dangerous outside world, filled with totalitarian wickedness trying to destroy the American way of life[4]. Trone appears to have been to Shipley public enemy number one, for reasons that were never actually stated.

She had become known as "the Czarina of the Potomac" by those who did not agree with her. Many objected to her zealous refusal of the right of travel to anyone who was a communist and or a friend of a communist, or a suspected communist, or even a suspected friend of a suspected communist[5]. When she revoked a passport it was final, there was no recourse to anyone else, and her word was the ultimate decision on the matter.

The door to her office was always open, and any applicant with a grievance could see that she was there and could walk right in. She had an inexhaustible amount of patience to hear requests for appeal but her answer was invariably no.

In 1932 however, Mrs. Ruth Bielaski Shipley was at the height of her power, and ready and willing to exercise it when she saw necessary. She had certain elements that directed her actions, that invariably when into her decision to either issue or revoke a passport. Sometimes the decision was based on information supplied by intelligence agencies. Of course Trone was a frequent name in the correspondence between the intelligence agencies and Ruth[6].

It appeared from intelligence reports that Trone was in fact working to get political opponents of the Nazis out of the camps, and not just the Jews. Angering Hitler and dragging America into a war was not on Ruth's agenda.

In 1932 when Trone became a citizen of the United States, and applied for a passport he may not have realized to whom he was applying. Although he initially got his passport, his name was specifically marked out by Ruth. She appeared to know that Trone was lying about his age[7].

By 1939 Ruth had been briefed about the accusation made about Trone in Jamaica several years before[8]. She was also receiving reports from the FBI regarding Trone as well at this time. When Trone applied to get a passport for the Dominican Republic project, he found his passport restricted to a limited number of countries, a restriction he ignored.

When Trone tried to get out of Washington in 1943, as the investigations intensified, he would run into substantial difficulties[9]. The Prime Minister of China and the U.S. State Department would beg Ruth to relent and give Trone a passport. There is a note this time in which Ruth tells the FBI that she may have to give Trone a passport because she is receiving substantial political pressure to do so. That Ruth would bend at all is a testament to the friends Trone had in high places.

As Trone travelled around the world avoiding the United States, Ruth could do nothing to stop him. As long as his passport did not expire, Trone was free from Ruth. In 1945 Trone was given a passport at the special request of the State Department because they needed him to help negotiate with the Soviets. These extensions of his passport and his continued support from powerful interests in the State Department and elsewhere stymied Ruth's ability to stop Trone.

In 1953 Ruth would finally get her chance to stop Trone. Having been fully briefed into the espionage investigations underway into Trone, Ruth felt at liberty to finally remove the passport of Trone. She had noticed that he was away working outside of the United States from 1943 to 1953. Trone was a naturalized U.S. citizen. Ruth decided therefore, in her inaccurate interpretation of the immigration law, that the absence constituted his giving up his citizenship.

The law of course said no such thing. In the note placed in Trone's file[10] Ruth laid out her reason why he should not have his passport renewed. The reasons were that he had spent too long outside of the country. Trone was no longer a citizen. As no one could challenge Ruth's authority at this time, the revocation of Trone's passport and citizenship was final.

At the age of 81 Trone would find that he was stranded in London England, where he was temporarily staying while his daughter was going to University there. When the U.S. embassy had informed him that he was no longer a citizen, according to the decision of the head of the Passport Office, Trone did not complain or ask for even the statement in writing. His wife Florence was puzzled by this and she, against the advice of her husband requested a written receipt that Trone's passport had been revoked[11].

By this time, the actions of the Passport Office must have appeared as a gift to everyone. No intelligence agency could make their mind up about Trone, nor did they wish him to go public with what he knew. Trone also did not see any reason to get back to the United States. As a non-status person in England Trone found that he could exist quite comfortably.

Trone at this time was functioning as an advice bureau for British Members of Parliament regarding such issues the atomic bomb and Israel. Trone had by this point made a significant number of contacts with the British Labour Party elite, and they in turn were relying on Trone for his advice on world politics and technical issues[12].

Some of Trone's Latvian relatives were also, by sheer chance, living in London as well. Surrounded by a growing number of friends and by relatives Trone had accidently found himself an environment where he could enjoy the benefits of a major international city, complete with its scientific and cultural institutions that he would enjoy extensively in the coming years.

There is as yet no evidence that Ruth Bielaski Shipley head of the Passport office acted under anyone's direction when she revoked Trone's passport and citizenship. Ruth had been determined to take Trone's passport for over a decade before this point, but had been stopped in her attempt. The only person to protest at Trone's passport being removed was a lawyer who usually represented the financial interests associated with some of the most rich and powerful Americans such as J. P. Morgan Junior. That person was Trone's friend Dick Scandrett. Dick acted alone, not at Trone's request and his appeal was entirely rejected by Ruth[13].

Questions & Answers

Who was Solomon Trone? He was born in Yelgava Latvia and died in Chianti Italy[14]. He was 97 when he died. It is doubtful that before seeing this book you will know anything about him, and yet all of our lives on the planet were in some way affected by his actions. As the world became divided up by ideologies, it was to some degree the life of Dr. Trone that ironically made it possible. Both the good and the bad of our times derive from the actions of those men who brought the modern age into existence in the dying days of World War One.

As the old empires collapsed and the European powers were reduced to shadows of their former power, the United States and the Soviet Union moved in to fill that vacuum of power. How they consolidated their power and how they developed their societies was built upon a new way of doing business, a new way of living; life as part of a technically planned and organized global community. Trone was the disciple of the technocrats he met in New York. What he helped bring into Russia was the technocratic faith, faith that new technology and adapting our lives to that technology could resolve the most difficult and important issues of contention.

Beyond the Soviet Union the technocratic movement spread out transcending borders, ideologies and a plethora of differences, reshaping the world. Trone was part of a movement that swept the world, he tirelessly worked to redesign and reshape life on the planet so that a planned rational community of man could develop. Few men have done so much for world development and have been so little acknowledged as to their contribution.

As we pass the anniversary of the 1917 October Revolution, an event fundamental to global development, we may start now to re-evaluate and re-imagine our ideals, the essential way we see the world through those ideals. The hegemonic power of Russia and America has been irreparably broken and the technocratic ideal has been in full retreat globally since 1968.

What Dr. Trone was able to do was inspire, to deeply understand the world he lived and to re-imagine that world as something better; built upon rational humane principles. What went wrong, what is our responsibility today to learn and do better, are all questions that must find inspiration and warning in what was done in the events of 1917.

Dr. Trone was an agent of change in the Modern world. His life and works should be studied to understand that change. In this book we can to the small degree possible in such a work understand and appreciate who he was and what he tried to achieve.

It is not the purpose of this work to pass the final judgement upon the life and works of Solomon Trone. Nor is it possible to offer a definitive history of Trone's life. Too much is unknown; too many historical events are defined by nothing more than speculation. It may never be possible to create a complete picture of the most important moments in Trone's life. What words did he exchange with Morgan if any? What was his exact connection to Lenin? Exactly how many did he save from destruction by the Nazis? The questions remaining are vast; the facts that are arranged in this work are small by comparison.

The hope for a greater understanding is to be found, if anywhere, in the pain staking work of academics and researchers engaged throughout the world in one large project to bring all the necessary pieces together. Where ever Dr. Trone worked, there we may find a clue to his elusive history. It is the hope in writing this work that it may illicit the attention of scholars around the globe in different fields. These scholars may it is hoped bring together the pieces of this puzzle that are scattered in the archives of many countries and corporate bodies.

Nowhere is our understanding of Trone more lacking than in the obscure motivations behind the agreements that were made between the Capitalists and Anti-Capitalists in the time between 1917 and 1953. To these agreements Trone was an integral and perhaps necessary component. Trone was never indiscreet either in matters of love or matters of business; therefore much is left unknown exactly as he desired it would be.

At the moment all that we owe to understanding Trone can be laid at the feet of Ilf and Petrov. As impossible as it may seem, it is only in the writings of a supposed fiction that we see the motivations of Trone laid bare. There we see Trone complete with all his dreams and ideals made visible, his fears and his hatreds given voice. Even Trone's tears and passions are given to us as real as if we witnessed them for ourselves all thanks to the tremendous literary abilities of Ilf and Petrov.

When Ilf and Petrov voyaged around America, they voyaged around Trone; they circumnavigated and mapped out the modern technocratic age. In describing Trone they inadvertently described so much of the age where global development became a unitary ideal, in which the world became one mass of understanding and struggle. They gave an understanding to what we now call Globalization.

Trone's life and philosophy was at the thematic core of the ideas so pervasive and so thoroughly debated at the time. Trone in many ways was the spirit of the age made flesh. The rise of the Technocratic world order, the globalization of life on the planet is not merely an abstract philosophical concept to be debated in universities; to Trone these represented his purpose in life. The events in his life from 1905 to 1953 were remarkably singular in their intent. His aim and life goal can only be summed up by a term he would not have been familiar with at the time, as its parlance is entirely contemporary with the time of this work's publication. That term is globalization.

As we all know the globalization of modern life has been conceived as a mixed blessing at best. Without the events and movements that Trone is most closely associated with this globalization of life on the planet would not have occurred. Whether such a process was inevitable or preventable Trone's perspective provides us a window on a world in crisis. Trone is seen in the midst of a great movement of change, no less spectacular and arguably more so than any other time of change for life on the planet.

The complexity of coordination of human endeavour on the planet reached a truly global level with Trone and his contemporaries. No longer was there a periphery and a center. There was one political economic structure whose interdependent functions could amass in a short time the production of goods and the destruction of life on such a scale that previously such actions would have taken centuries.

Trone and his fellow technocrats are largely responsible for this colossal world of possibilities. Before the 20th century we as a planet could not produce enough food to feed ourselves. Now we produce three times more food than we need. At the beginning of the twentieth century we were dependent upon non-renewable fuels, now we could if we wished entirely sustain ourselves with renewable energy resources such as solar, tidal, geothermal, and wind power.

Before the twentieth century the science of medicine was little more than the elixir of hope and had little positive or negative effect upon the longevity of human life. The rampant diseases that shortened life the 19th century, now in the 21st century present no practical problems in their complete eradication.

Perhaps the most stunning of all developments is the complete destruction of Western European Empires. At the end of the 19th century these empires held monolithic centralized power over the mass of humanity over the entire planet. They also appeared indestructible. Now those empires are mere memories.

How this happened as we have seen through the life of Trone can be directly linked to the events of 1917. What those events successfully challenged was not the autocracy of Russia in so much as the way the world went about the business of industry before that point. What it was able to establish was a new way of doing business, the new global political economy of the day.

To say the technocratic movement was a failure is to see things through the wrong end of the telescope. The problems we face today are not strictly speaking the result of the aims of Technocrats of whom Trone is perhaps their most foremost example. If we can at all lay the problems of our age at the feet of the Technocrats and Trone in particular, it is in that their aims were too narrow. So narrow and limited were their goals, of providing to the world greater technical efficiency, that they would work tirelessly for those in power who would eventually be their executioners.

Lenin, Stalin, Truman, and Chang Kai Chek all directly benefited from employing Trone in their interests. Trone of course worked for each of them with the same good humour, intelligence and enthusiasm. Trone would appear to be in the ranks of such amoral and apolitical technocrats as Werner Von Braun and Robert S. McNamara; following the orders of political leaders whose political aims they neither agree nor disagree.

This picture of Trone the scientist or engineer who just wanted to do his job and not mind the consequences, does however omit one key detail. Trone was not a scientist, nor was he particularly known for his engineering abilities. He knew people, knew how to talk to people and was able to bring out and represent the ideas of others. Trone first and foremost brought people together, brought ideas together and was able to bring the disparate elements of a troubled planet into a common understanding.

We make our plans for the future and then those plans make us what we are. This was the essence of Trone's work. He helped people as a group come to decisions about the future. Trone was not of course always successful, and many of the decisions people came up with have proven to be disasters. He tried to make sure that the new technology when implemented would correspond to how we wanted our societies to be; encapsulating our cultures, our dreams, our hopes and our fears.

The technology was supposed to, through proper planning, represent the interests of society. Representing society's interests or rather the interests of those who held power in those societies, inevitably made society more of what it was at that time. A fixed point of social development and inequality had been writ large into a future world. The plan was no more than a set of relations that would replicate the exact wishes of a political and economic elite into the future on a global scale.

It is important to ask the question therefore, in whose interest did Trone create his plans? To this question there is unfortunately no straight answer. In his work he tried to represent everyone, going as deep and wide in his investigations as he could. This was the work he loved, talking to people, finding out as much as he could. His abilities in this regard were phenomenal, as the work of Ilf and Petrov can attest.

Trone did not feel the need to examine in detail what he had done, and its consequences. Trone was given many opportunities to write his life story. At one point a publisher offered him a tape recorder and said they would publish whatever he had to say. Trone refused the offer. For Trone, it could be said, there was only the future that mattered, a future that could be read in the seemingly endless series of plans that he authored.

Trone was working for a future vision of society, one that did not exist except in his imagination drawn from the possibilities nascent within the material conditions of the world he investigated. The disasters of the present, the danger and drama were unable to penetrate and pierce the bubble of a possible future world. He could see beyond the present, and lived almost entirely imagining what could be instead of dwelling on what was.

To place Trone and position him in the web of complex political relations between communist and capitalist, east and west is to miss the essential aspect of Trone's life. What began in the blood bath of 1905's massacre was Trone's commitment to political action. It placed him in a series of intense political dramas that in turn moved him to the center of great historical events. As Trone however had committed himself to political action he had also never given up his imaginative creativity and his love of company and conversation.

Trone was always the dreamer and the lover of humanity, but events had so played out that he was forced time and again to face the catastrophic realities of the twentieth century. Trone was a curious combination of a man faced with a series of mass tragedies of humanity and yet one who would not allow himself to be consumed by those events. Because of this curious ability of Trone people in the most desperate situations relied on him to do what no one else could.

Quite simply Trone did not know when to quit. He refused to be defeated. In the depths of the massacre in 1905 part of Trone had died with those he loved. What died within Trone was the belief that he could simply do nothing. He had to engage life, and engage it he did. He could never turn back and be silent and do nothing in the face of injustice.

Does this justify his work with the political elite whose crimes Trone was well aware of? No it does not but it does in large measure explain rightly or wrongly why he did it. He made his decisions with eyes wide open albeit with perhaps somewhat more optimism than was warranted. Yet it was that optimism that kept him going; like a modern day and real life Candide.

It is a life unfortunately that is not known due to a lack of any published biography. This was much to the lament of people who knew him. The scientist and scholar Joseph Needham who knew Trone very well sent a letter to Florence Trone upon hearing about his death:

> Did you ever manage to get him to jot down a few notes from which you might compile an autobiography? We do hope so, because we think it would be wonderful if there could be some sort of publication to record his wonderful life. He was really a great figure of the "third world," always so enthusiastic about the possibilities of the under-developed countries and the great capabilities of their peoples, if only the economic difficulties could be overcome. He

must have been a great inspiration to many besides ourselves, and we would like to think that there could be some general recognition of this[15].

His allegiances were to the ideals of his fallen comrades in 1905. His love and passion for life was that of a man who lives in immediate expectation of death, and yet tried to make every minute count. Quite simply he lived outside of his time and place and in the world of ideals and future possibilities. His mission was to change the future direction of the world so that it fit those higher ideals. To complete his mission he needed talk to everyone; to bring everyone together in one massive plan for a future world.

The two great writers Ilf and Petrov understood Trone better than anyone. It is therefore fitting that for the last word on Solomon Trone we should turn to them. For them Trone could be encapsulated in how he saw the world.

(Trone) was very absent-minded. Yet his was not the traditional meek absent-mindedness of a scientist, but rather the stormy, aggressive absent-mindedness of a healthy person full of curiosity carried away by a conversation or a thought and for the time being forgetting the rest of the world[16].

Endnotes

1   (Weyl 2003)
2   (Weyl 2003)
3   (Hoover, FBI J. E. Hoover to State Dept. 1949)
4   (The Administration: Sorry, Mrs. Shipley 1951)
5   (Passport to Politics 1955)
6   (Passport Division 1932-1965)
7   (Passport Division 1932-1965)
8   (The Marcus Garvy and the Universal Negro Improvement Association Papers 1990)
9   (China Defense Supply 1943-1945)
10   (Passport Division 1932-1965)
11   (Trone, et al. 2009)
12   (Trone, et al. 2009)
13   (Trone, et al. 2009)
14   (F. Trone 1969)
15   (Needham December15, 1969)
16   (Ilf and Petrov 1937, 105)

BIBLIOGRAPHY

Amelia R. Fry; Regional Oral History Office, University of California, Berkeley. "Speaker for Suffrage and Petitioner for Peace." *Suffragists Oral History Project; Mabel Vernon Interview 1976* . 2011. http://content.cdlib.org/view?docId=k-t2r29n5pb&brand=calisphere (accessed 12 12, 2017).

Bailes, Kendall E. "The Politics of Technology: Stalin and Technocratic Thinking among Soviet Engineers." *The American Historical Review, Vol. 79, No. 2*, April 1974: 445-469.

Bailes, Kendalle E. "The American Connection: Ideology and the Transfer of American Technology to the Soviet Union, 1917-1941." *Comparative Studies in Society and History, Vol. 23, No. 3.*, July 1981: 421-448.

Bielaski, Alexander Bruce. "Correspondence to Roland Ford, concerning the matter of Congressman Lunn's accusation of Trone as an agent of the Imperial Government of Russia and the Romanoff Royal Family." November 9, 1917.

Boyd, Peter. "William Corcoran, U.S. Diplomat and War II Spy, Dead." *Washington Post*, September 11, 1962.

Breitman, Richard. "The Allied War Effort and the Jews, 1942-1943 ." *Journal of Contemporary History, Vol. 20, No. 1, Jan., 1985*, 1985: 135-156.

Brysac, Shareen Blair. *Resisting Hitler: Mildred Harnack and the Red Ochestra.* 2000.

Business Historical Society. "When I got out of law school, I went to work for a law firm and began running errands. I have been running other people's errands ever since." *Bulletin of the Business Historical Society, Vol. 11, No. 5*, November, 1937: 97.

Canadian Immigration Agent Inspection. "Port of Landing." Victoria, Canada, May 28, 1917.

Chernow, Ron. *The House of Morgan: An American Banking Dynasty and the Rise of Modern Finance.* 2001.

China Defense Supply. "Correspondence, (1943-1945)." 1943-1945.

Congress of Women at The Hague. "International Congress of Women; Appendix 3." *Women at The Hague* . New York: Macmillan, 1915. 72-77.

Department of State. "Passport Application: C. H. Minor." February 26, 1918.

—. "Passport Application: Gerard Swope." April 19, 1917.

—. "Passport Application: Gerard Swope." 1915.

—. "Passport Application: Maurice Oudin." January 11, 1917.

—. "Passport Application: Perkins." December 14, 1916.

Dorn, Harold. "Hugh Lincoln Cooper and the First Détente." *Technology and Culture, Vol. 20, No. 2*, April 1979: 322-347.

Engerman, David C. . "Economic Reconstruction in Soviet Russia: The Courting of Herbert Hoover in 1922." *The International History Review, Vol. 19, No. 4 (Nov., 1997)*, 1997: 836-847.

Fawcett, Brian C. "Chinese Labour Detachment." *Journal of the Hong Kong Branch of the Royal Asiatic Society vol. 40*, 2000: 68.

Federal Bureau of Investigation. "1951 04 10 FBI NYFile 100-96127." Investigation, New York, 1951.

Federal Bureau of Investigation. "FBI Investigation FILE 77-58706 William J. Donovan (1953)." Investigation, 1953.

Federal Bureau of Investigation. "Name Check (July 25, 1949)." 1949.

—. "Reparations Committee FBI Investigation." *FOIAPA FBI-77-27252 Vol. 2*. 10 19, 1945.

Federal Bureau of Investigations. "1950 02 09 FBI NYFile 100-96127." Investigation, New York, 1950.

Federal Bureau of Investigations. "1950 06 20 FBI NYFile 100-96127." Investigation, New York, 1950.

Federal Bureau of Investigations. "1950 12 07 FBI File 100-96127." Investigation, 1950.

Federal Bureau of Investigations. "1951 02 10 FBI NYFile 100-96127." Investigation, New York, 1951.

Federal Bureau of Investigations. "FBI Wash File 100-21210." Washington, January 12, 1951.

Federal Bureau of Investigations. "FBI Investigation Subject Trone." 1917-1921.

Federal Bureau of Investigations. "FBI NYFile 100-96127." New York, August 25, 1950.

Federal Bureau of Investigations. "Matter of Trone – European Neutrality Matter." Investigation, November 9, 1917 – November 7, 1920.

Federal Bureau of Investigations. "NY File 100-96127, (June 16, 1951)." Investigation, New York, 1951.

—. "SAC to FBI Director." June 20, 1950.

Flaningam, M. L. "International Co-operation and Control in the Electrical Industry: The General Electric Company and Germany, 1919-1944." *American Journal of Economics and Sociology, Vol. 5, No. 1 Oct., 1945*, 1945: 7-25.

Frieden, Jeff. "Sectoral Conflict and Foreign Economic Policy, 1914-1940." *International Organization, The State and American Foreign Economic Policy Vol. 42, No. 1*, Winter, 1988: 59-90.

Friedman, Saul S. *No haven for the oppressed ; United States policy toward Jewish refugees, 1938-1945*. Detroit: Wayne State University Press, 1973.

General Electric . " Correspondence regarding the citizenship application of Solomon Trone." Schenectady Museum and Archives, 1925.

Godine, David R. "Owen D. Young: An American Enterprise ." Boston: Case and Case, 1982.

Goldman, Emma. "Address to the Jury by Emma Goldman, Delivered during her Anti-Conscription trial, New York City, July 9, 1917." *The Emma Goldman Papers, Berkeley Library University of California*. 1917. http://www.lib.berkeley.edu/goldman/pdfs/Speeches-AddresstotheJury.pdf (accessed December 12, 2017).

—. "What I Believe." *New York World*, July 19, 1908.

Goldstein, Mark L. " Washington and the Networks of W. W. Corcoran ." *Business and Economic History Vol. 5*, 2007.

Hamerow, Theodore S. *Why We Watched By*. W.W. Norton, 2009.

Handlin, Oscar. "A Russian Anarchist Visits Boston." *The New England Quarterly, Vol. 15, No. 1.*, March 1942: 104-109.

Harvard University Archives: Papers of Thomas Hill, biographical notes. October 14, 2016 . http://oasis.lib.harvard.edu/oasis/deliver/~hua15005 (accessed October 12, 2017).

Harvard University. "Dedication of the Thomas Nelson Perkins Room." Harvard, 1941.

"Havoc Wrought In Morgan Offices." *The New York Times*. New York , September 1, 1920.

Hindustan Times (New Delhi, India). "Mr. Trone Arriving in August." July 24, 1949.

Hoff, Joan. *Ideology and Economics*. 1974.

Hoover, J. E. "Correspondence J. E. Hoover to State Department and CIA." Investigation, June 13, 1950.

—. "FBI Correspondence to Nicholson." March 30, 1951.

—. "FBI J. E. Hoover Regarding Trone." March 12, 1958.

—. "FBI J. E. Hoover to State Dept." December 21, 1949.

Il'f, Ilia. *Ilia Il'f Zapisnie knizki 1925 - 1937, Pervoe polnoe izdanie, Commentaries(notes)*. Edited by Alexadra Il'f. Moscow: Moskva "Tekst," 2000.

Ilf, Ilya, and Eugene Petrov. *Little Golden America*. New York: Farrar & Rinehart, 1937.

J. P. Morgan, Jr. 1867-1943. University Press of Virgnia, 1981.

Jaffe, Julian F. . In *Crusade Against Radicalism, New York During The Red Scare, 1914-1924*, 176-177. Port Washington, New York, London: National University Publications, 1972.

Who Shall Live And Who Shall Die? . Directed by Laurence Jarvik. 1981.

Johnston, Charles. "Sergé Iulitch Witté ." *The North American Review, Vol. 181, No. 586*, September 1905: 435-447.

Kuromiya, Hiroaki. "The Soviet Famine of 1932-1933 Reconsidered." *Europe-Asia Studies, Vol. 60, No. 4*, June 2008: 663-675.

Lenin, Vladimir Ilych . *Imperialism, The Highest Stage of Capitalism*. Zurich, 1916.

Lenin, Vladimir. *Report on the Work of the Council of People's Commissars*. Moscow: Political Report of the CC,[2] Polnoe sobranie sochinenii, 5th edn (Moscow, 1975-9) vol 36, 15-16, December 22, 1920.

Loth, D. *The Story of Gerard Swope and General Electric in American Business*. 1958.

"Meeting Senator Marshall and S. A. Trone." October 15, 1948.

Meyer, B. H. "Foreign Railway Events in 1902-03 ." *Annals of the American Academy of Political and Social Science*, January 1904: 121-140.

"Morgan." In *Concise Dictionary of American Biography*, 839-841. American Council of Learned Societies, 1971.

Musk, George. *A Short History and Fleet List of the Canadian Pacific Ocean Steamships: 1891 - 1961*. London, 1961.

Nair, Kusum. "Attitudes and Latitudes, (August 27, 1950)." *India magazine*, 1950.

Needham, Joseph. "Correspondence of Joseph Needham to Florence Trone." Cambridge, England, December15, 1969.

Nehru, Jawaharlal. "Introduction to M. R. Masani, Soviet Sidelights (1936), rpt." In *Selected Works Jawaharlal Nehru*, by Jawaharlal Nehru, 7: 128-129. New Dehli, India, 1972.

—. *Toward Freedom: The Autobiography of J. Nehru.* New York, 1941.

New York Sun. "Big Bang on Wall Street." September 6, 1920.

New York Time. "Solomon Trone pictured in the photograph of courtroom spectators." December 14, 1930.

"Passenger Manifest: Empress of Russia." San Francisco, 1917.

Passport Division. "Mrs. Shipley Correspondence ." 1932-1965.

Podpali, Victor. "Political Last Will and Testament of Victor Podpali." January 28, 1931.

Rabushka, Dr. Alvin. *The Director's Column, IASPS Quarterly Report.* IASPS , Winter 2001.

Reich, Leonard S. "Lighting the Path to Profit: G.E.'s Control of the Electric Lamp Industry, 1892-1941,." *The Business History Review, Vol. 66, No. 2. (Summer, 1992)*, 1992: 305-334.

Rogger, Hans. "Amerikanizm and the Economic Development of Russia." *Comparative Studies in Society and History, Vol. 23, No. 3.* , July 1981: 382-420.

Ross, Nicholas. "Sosua: A Colony of Hope." *American Jewish History, Vol. 82 No. 1-4*, 1994.

Roth, Andrew. "Mr. Point Four." *The Nation*, January 27, 1951: 83.

Rothschild, William E. *The Secret to G.E.'s Success.* New York, 2007.

S. A. Trone Business Agent, International General Electric Schenectady, N.Y. - suspected Radical, Testimony of Minorsky, D. F. Broderick. Albany N.Y.: FBI Report, September 11, 1920.

Scheiber, Harry N. "World War I as Entrepreneurial Opportunity: Willard Straight and the American International Corporation." *Political Science Quarterly, Vol. 84, No. 3* , September 1969: 486-511.

Schmidt, Barbara. "..knife a Romanoff wherever you find him... Mark Twain On Czars, Siberia And The Russian Revolution." 2008.

Seaburg, Carl, and Stanley Paterson. *Merchant Prince of Boston. Colonel T.H. Perkins, 1764-1854 .* 1971.

Seagrave, Sterling. *The Soong Dynasty.* Harper and Row , 1985.

Simms, J. Y. "The Economic Impact of the Russian Famine of 1891-92." *The Slavonic and East European Review, Vol. 60, No. 1* , January 1982: 63-74.

Smalley, Eugene Virgil. *History of the Northern Pacific Railroad, , 1841-1899.* 1981.

Smith, Richard Harris. *OSS: A Secret History.* University of California Press, 1982.

SS Flandre. "Passenger List." September 11, 1914.

Steinmetz, Charles Proteus. *America and the New Epoch.* New York, August 1916.

Stetler, Russell D. "Freedom To Travel." *Left and Right 2, No. 2 (Spring 1966)*, 1966: 58-72.

Swope, Gerard, interview by Columbia University Library Collections. *Reminiscences of Gerard Swope* (1953).

Swope, Gerrard. "Correspondence regarding Trone reference." February 24, 1939.

Swope, Henrietta Hill. "Swope, Henrietta Hill, 1902-1982. 76-84: Travel: plans, itineraries, correspondence, diaries 76. "China and Japan, 1917"; includes diary. Schlesinger Library, Radcliffe Institute." 1917.

Temin, Peter. "Soviet and Nazi Economic Planning in the 1930s." *The Economic History Review, New Series, Vol. 44, No. 4* , November, 1991: 573-593.

The American Jewish Joint Distribution Committee. "Correspondence to Ruth Shipley Passport Division." New York City, 1939-1941.

The Marcus Garvy and the Universal Negro Improvement Association Papers. "Outlines Solomon Trones visit to Jamaica and his meeting with Marcus Garvey." 1990.

The New York Times. "Aunt of U. S. Consul Dies In Exiles' Camp." February 21, 1941: 4.

The New York Times. "Bruce Bielaski, Justice Aide, Dies." February 20, 1964: 29.

The New York Times. "Corporation Reports." October 15, 1929: 57.

The New York Times. "Emily Delafield Engaged to Wed." 1926.

The New York Times. "Intruder Has Dynamite." 7 4, 1915: 1.

The New York Times. "Iron Slugs Pierce Wall." 7 6, 1915: 1.

The New York Times. "Married." December 31, 1896.

The New York Times. "Minor Dies." February 5, 1967.

The New York Times. "Mr. T. N. Perkins An American's Public Service." October 26, 1937.

The New York Times. "Mrs. Oudin Obituary." July 8, 1956.

The New York Times. "Obituary Notice." July 8, 1928.

The New York Times. "Perkins Called "Leading Citizen of Country," Praised for His Devoted Service and Public Spirit by Fellow Officers." October 8, 1937.

The New York Times. "Perkins Defends Late J. P. Morgan." April 12, 1915: 5.

The New York Times. "Plans Laid to Trade with Russia." March 20, 1934.

The New York Times. "Savage - Oudin." 1926.

The New York Times. "Soviet Envoy Host At Brilliant Fete." April 11, 1934: 14.

The New York Times. "Yesterday's Weddings." 10 12, 1892.

Thomas, G. Cary. *Memoir of T. H. Perkins.* 1856.

Time. "The Administration: Sorry, Mrs. Shipley." December 31, 1951.

Times Herald. "Passport to Politics." March 3, 1955: 14.

Trone, Alexandra. "Email Correspondance S. Trone." London, UK, Decmeber 15, 2007.

Trone, Dimitri. "Correspondence to Hall of History Committee." June 15, 1978.

Trone, Florence. "Correspondence from Florence Trone to Joseph Needham." Poggiolino, Greve chianti, Florence, Italy, December 5, 1969.

The American Who Electrified Russia - (Including research conducted for film as research archivist). Directed by Michael Chanan. Performed by Sasha Trone, et al. 2009.

Trone, Solomon. "Biographical statement regarding passport." August 14, 1953.

Trone, Solomon. "Brief Outline of my Engineering Experience." Biographical, Delhi, India, 1949.

Trone, Solomon. "Brief Sketch." Biographical, Paris, France, July 26, 1950.

—. "Confidential correspondence Trone to Nehru." 1949, November 21, 1949.

—. "Correspondence from Trone to Carwell." February 14, 1950.

—. "Correspondence from Trone to Swope." Paris, France, January 19, 1939.

—. "Correspondence to Yin, (November 12, 1945)." November 12, 1945.

—. "FBI application - Lend Lease ." February 1, 1943.

—. "General Electric Director's Records (Solomon Trone)Фонд 1367. Опись 8. Дело 1051 / Фонд 1367. Опись 8. Дело 1022 / ЦГИА. Фонд 1367. Опись 4. Дело 76." St. Petersburg, Russian Federation: St. Petersburg Historical Archive Russia, 1916-1918.

Trone, Solomon. *General Report on Taiwan, unpublished manuscript submitted to the National Resources Commission.* Nanking, China: National Resources Commission, 21 January 1948.

Trone, Solomon. "German Payments: Basic Development Programme (for Israel)." Tel Aviv, 1952.

—. "Israeli Survey Workbook for Development Programme Report." 1951.

—. "Letter Regarding Famine Relief, China." October 17, 1948.

Trone, Solomon, interview by USA Consulate in Riga Estonia. *State Department Solomon Trone Interview* (March 15, 1933).

Trone, Solomon. "Statement." Biographical, London England, August 14, 1953.

—. " On the Volga, Letters to the Editor." *The Nation*, October 1, 1934 .

U.S. Census. "Oudin." 1880.

United Electrical, Radio and Machine Workers of America. "Nasty Business: Corporate Deals and Nazi Germany." *Nasty Nazi Business: Corporate Deals with Nazi Germany.* 2003. (accessed December 12, 2017).

Van Kleeck . "Correspondence with Solomon Trone, (1935- 1943)." 1935- 1943.

Wagner, Heather Lehr, and Tara Baukus Mello. *The Central Intelligence Agency.* 2007.

Wang, Hong-zen. "Class Structures and Social Mobility in Taiwan in the Initial Post-War Period ." *The China Journal, No. 48.* , July, 2002: 55-85.

Washington Post. "Men Whose Lives Have Been Sought By Bomb Plotters." May 1, 1919: 1.

Washington Post. "Paul D. Boyd, William Corcoran, U.S. Diplomat and War II Spy, Dead." September 11, 1962: B4.

Washington Post. "Relief Goes To Siberia." December 19, 1916: 3.

Washington Post. "Transfers." June 11, 1939.

Wasserstein, Bernard. *Britain and the Jews of Europe, 1939-1945 .* London: Institute of Jewish Affairs, 1979.

Wells, Allen. *Tropical Zion.* Duhram and London: Duke University Press, 2009.

Weyl, Nathanial. *Encounters with Communism.* 2003.

Wikipedia. *American International Corporation .* 23 February 2011 г. https://ru.wikipedia.org/wiki/American_International_Corporation (дата обращения: 2 October 2017 г.).

Zahavi, Gerald. "Passionate Commitments: Race, Sex, and Communism at Schenectady General Electric, 1932-1954." *The Journal of American History, Vol. 83, No. 2.*, September, 1996: 514-548.

Zvielli, Alexander. "The Jewish hush-hush policy." *Jerusalem Post*, April 17, 2009.